BRIDGES TO A BRIGHTER FUTURE

BRIDGES TO A
BRIGHTER FUTURE

FULFILLING OUR PURPOSE AND TRANSFORMING OUR SOCIETY

DR. MARCUS BRIGHT

DEDICATION

To all those who dare to dream and envision a brighter future, whose aspirations inspire hope and ignite change, this book is dedicated to you. May it serve as a guiding light along your path, empowering you to fulfill your purpose and reminding you of the immense potential within you.

Together, let us bridge the gaps that divide us, connecting hearts, minds, and communities as we strive for a society where justice, equality, and opportunity thrive.

TABLE OF CONTENTS

PREFACE

*B*ridges to a Brighter Future: Fulfilling Our Purpose and Transforming Our Society provides insight, information, and inspiration to help people achieve their individual goals and make meaningful contributions to the broader progress that we can make as a society.

The book delves into the urgent need to disrupt the school-to-prison pipeline and advance economic opportunity for all. I address the systemic barriers that perpetuate inequality and offer tangible solutions on a structural level. By combining policy changes with grassroots initiatives and community engagement, I write about a society where equitable access to quality education and economic opportunities is available to everyone.

Through my own experiences and the power of human connections, I emphasize the importance of bridges that provide opportunities, knowledge, and different perspectives. By recognizing our interconnectedness and mobilizing our collective strengths, we can address pressing societal issues and bring about transformation. In this book, I invite you on a journey of self-discovery, personal growth, and societal transformation for the betterment of all. I challenge you to explore your own purpose and use it as a driving force for personal and collective progression.

CHAPTER ONE

BRIDGES TO A BRIGHTER FUTURE

As you begin this book, you are embarking on a transformative adventure guided by the belief that every individual has the power to shape their destiny. Within these pages, we will delve into the essence of a brighter future. What does your brighter future look like? It looks different for all of us, but in this book, I put forth a common definition of a brighter future, and that is the fulfillment of your purpose—the fulfillment of your calling. For some, it could be the fulfillment of a big dream that you have.

I believe that our dreams and purpose are connected. I believe that you find your purpose, you discover your calling in the dreams that have been embedded in you, in the impulses and inclinations that drive you. You find it in the interests and ambitions that have been placed in your heart and mind.

Each one of us has been bestowed with unique talents, abilities, and qualities that make us special. These gifts are not random happenstances, but rather divine blessings given to us by a higher power. They are like seeds planted within us, waiting to be nurtured and brought to fruition.

Identifying our God-given gifts is a journey of self-discovery, a process that requires introspection, reflection, and an open heart. It is about understanding who we truly are at our core and recognizing the spark of greatness that resides within us. By exploring our passions, interests, and natural inclinations, we can begin to uncover the hidden treasures that have been bestowed upon us.

Once we have identified our gifts, the next step is to understand our purpose. Our purpose is the reason why we are here on this earth, the unique mission that only we can fulfill. It is the intersection of our gifts, passions, and the needs of the world around us.

Discovering our purpose brings a profound sense of fulfillment, joy, and meaning to our lives. It gives us a sense of direction and guides our decisions and actions. When we align our lives with our purpose, we tap into a limitless source of energy, motivation, and inspiration. We become vessels through which our gifts can create positive change in the world.

But why is it so crucial to identify our God-given gifts and purpose? The answer lies in the impact we can have on others and the world around us. When we live in alignment with our true selves, we radiate authenticity and attract opportunities that enable us to make a difference. Our gifts are not meant to be kept hidden but rather shared with the world to uplift and empower others.

Moreover, when we embrace our gifts and purpose, we become living testimonies of the beauty and potential that exists within each human being. We inspire others to embark on their own journey of self-discovery and encourage them to uncover their unique gifts. In doing so, we create a ripple effect of positive change that can transform lives, communities, and even the world at large.

So, I urge each one of you to embark on this journey of self-discovery, to delve deep within yourselves and recognize the extraordinary gifts you have been given. Embrace your purpose and let it guide you towards a life of fulfillment and impact. You are here for a reason, and your gifts have the power to shape the world in ways unimaginable.

I encourage you as you read this to pause for a few minutes, close your eyes and visualize your dream. Visualize you fulfilling a big dream that you have. Imagine yourself standing at the threshold of your greatest dream. Feel the excitement and anticipation coursing through your veins as you step into a world where your aspirations come to life. Picture every detail vividly, from the sights and sounds to the emotions you experience in that moment.

Why is visualization so important? It is because what we see in our minds has a profound impact on what we can achieve in reality. By visualizing our dreams, we activate our subconscious mind and align our energy toward manifesting our desired future.

Having a vision of realizing your dream and, even further, of fulfilling a higher purpose for yourself and the bigger impact that you want to make in this World is key because what you visualize today, you actualize in the future. This is the "brighter future" that I referred to earlier.

Remember, a brighter future is not merely about achieving personal success; it's about making a meaningful impact on the world around us. By visualizing our dreams and aligning them with a higher purpose, we become catalysts for positive change. We become bridges that connect dreams to reality, creating a ripple effect that extends far beyond ourselves.

Having this bigger vision of a brighter future helps you to align your focus. Where your focus goes, your energy goes. When I speak in different places, I often ask audiences who they think won the fight between the eagle and the snake. Most people say the eagle because of its aerial advantage and the fact that it can see a lot more and fly. I often surprise them when I say that the snake won. Why? Because the eagle shouldn't have been down there fighting in the first place. The eagle can fly and has no need to stoop down and fight with snakes. There are some battles that you have to fight, even if you lose. There are some battles that aren't worth fighting, even if you win.

It is now time to begin our journey to a brighter future. The journey goes over four different bridges that are key to the fulfillment of one's purpose. Each bridge is an essential component of the journey. The lessons that you gain from each bridge you carry on with you to the next bridge.

THE BELIEF BRIDGE

"All things are possible if you believe." – Mark 9:23

The first bridge is the belief bridge. If everyone is on your side, but you're not on your side, they can't help you. But if everyone is against you, but you believe in yourself, no one can stop you. Many of us have gifts, but we don't have enough belief in them. We have the competence, but we don't have the confidence.

Believe in and value your pathway. To get over the belief bridge, stories or narratives that are connected to your brighter future and that are in alignment with the higher vision for your life must win the belief battles and become dominant.

Some examples of belief battles are faith vs. fear, "I am inadequate" vs. "I am more than enough," and "I will always be in this bad circumstance" vs. "I am just one opportunity away from changing everything." You have the power of definition. Those who define you can confine you. You have agreement agency. You have the power to choose whether or not to make agreement with anything that comes your way.

A great example of someone who exercised his agreement agency to fight off the limiting beliefs that people had about him was Baltimore Ravens Quarterback Lamar Jackson. Despite winning the Heisman Trophy at the University of Louisville, many of the professional experts and prognosticators said that he could never be a quarterback in the NFL. They labeled him as only being a running back or a wide receiver at the next level in large part because he was a great runner. It also may have been assumed that he didn't have the intelligence, the throwing accuracy, or the capacity to be able to read an NFL defense at a high level.

They said that he did not have what it takes to be a quarterback, much less a starter, much less the MVP. Jackson didn't let those people define him, but he made up his own mind that he could be an elite quarterback and had confidence in his ability. He had an MVP belief in himself when others said that he wasn't even good enough to play in the league, and it manifested in real life a few years later.

He destroyed the boundaries that others tried to set for him and utilized tremendous self-confidence to break out of the parameters that were drawn for him. What Jackson used to fight off limiting beliefs in football, you can use to nullify other people's negative opinions about you in other areas of life. You don't have to be locked into existing narratives. They can be changed. New beliefs can become dominant and cause new actions to displace old practices.

The challenge is to not be controlled by the beliefs of others and to develop an inner peace that external factors cannot alter. Know who you are and remain grounded in that regardless of the location or people you are around. You must be stronger than the environment that you go in. Go in with a purpose that you don't deviate from.

Our society is set up to try to categorize people and put them into boxes. There are constant external evaluation and validation forces that can press on you. People will declare you as a winner or loser if you allow it to. You have the power to elect yourself as the President of your own environment. You have the power of agency and self-governance unless you decide to give it away. The choice is yours.

There is a need to examine the narratives that have risen to prominence and have gained a foothold in our individual and societal psyche. Some people push certain narratives because they feel like they validate who they are. The imagery that is depicted about certain kinds of people in the media not only plays a big role in shaping the external narratives of how they are seen, but it also impacts how people see themselves. These narratives can be internalized and affect both the way that people act and the way that they are treated.

There can be a whole host of associations that are attached to individuals or groups based on stereotypes that are derived from derogatory narratives. The more a narrative is repeated, the higher the likelihood that it will be internalized and broadly disseminated. When we relinquish that power, when we are completely reliant on the validation of other people — the external gaze — for our self-esteem, we put our value in a very vulnerable state.

The gaze is the external evaluation or judgment that people feel from others and the broader society at large. The fear of being judged is something that everyone must contend with to a certain extent. A key internal question to ask yourself is: are you doing what you are doing because you really want to, or are you doing it solely to get approval from the gaze?

There can be a continual search for validation and proving oneself as "worthy" in the eyes of those one sees as a "validator." These validators have been given power over some portion of the person's sense of self-worth. There is no doubt that there are members of the gaze who will matter more than others, like your significant other, children, and parents, but even the views of these loved ones can be detrimental if they exceed the power of your own definition of yourself. The power that the gaze has is in direct correlation to how much power you give to certain people to define who you are and the value that you possess.

You can create your own metrics. There is pressure to conform to society's metrics, and there can be a subsequent feeling of inferiority that accompanies it. In a world where comparison is rampant, and judgment is often harsh, no one wants to be made to feel inferior. However, it is all too common for others to try to impose their own standards upon us, seeking to put us in a subordinated status.

Society bombards us with measures of success — be it wealth, social status, appearance, or achievements. It attempts to convince us that these are the metrics we need to adhere to in order to be deemed valuable or worthy. Yet, please be reminded that your true worth cannot be quantified or determined by these superficial benchmarks. We have the power and the agency to define our own worth, irrespective of external judgments and expectations. We must never forget that.

We are all unique, with our own set of skills, talents, and passions. Embracing our individuality and celebrating our own strengths is an act of defiance against the pressures to conform. It is a declaration that we refuse to be confined within someone else's metrics. We don't have to succumb to society's judgments; we can rise above them.

How many of us have let somebody talk us out of our dreams? How many of us have buried our gifts and not pursued a big opportunity because we are afraid of criticism, perceived humiliation, or being disliked? I call this the disease of people-pleasing. John Lydgate is quoted as saying what Abraham Lincoln brought into greater prominence: "You can please some of the people all the time, all of the people some of the time, but you can't please all of the people all of the time."

The root cause of people pleasing lies in the fear of being disliked. It becomes a psychological prison of limiting beliefs that prevent people from truly living their best lives. By constantly seeking approval and validation from others, they sacrifice their own dreams, goals, and true passions.

But let me ask you this — is it truly worth it? Is it worth sacrificing your own calling, your own unique path in life? Is it worth living a life filled with regret, watching your true potential slip away? Your current situation does not dictate your potential. You are capable of so much more than you realize. Allow yourself to dream big, for it is through dreaming that we discover our true purpose and unlock our untapped potential.

You don't have to share your dream with everyone or get everyone's approval to make moves toward your dream. Society often places expectations and boundaries, dictating how far we should reach and what our aspirations should be.

There are those who have drawn a box for your life, and they will become infuriated if you dare to step out of the limitations, out of the confines that they believe that you should stay in. In the Bible, Joseph's own brothers tried to kill him because he shared his dream. He was cast into a pit and left for dead. Yet, he emerged stronger than ever, ultimately becoming a ruler in Egypt—a testament to the power of unwavering faith in one's dream.

Many of Dr. Martin Luther King Jr.'s fellow black leaders were jealous of him because of his dream, and many more white racists hated him even more because of it. Even amidst these challenges, he fought tirelessly, refusing to let anyone deter him from his mission of equality and justice. His dream resonated with millions, inspiring a nation and shaping history.

If you can't handle people getting mad at you for your dream, trying to talk you out of your dream, or feeling threatened by your dream, then keep it to yourself. Protect it. Nourish it. You don't have to share your dream with everyone or seek everyone's approval to make strides towards its realization.

If God has given you this dream, then you do not require anyone else's approval. You and God are a majority and an unstoppable force. The path to fulfilling your dreams may not be easy. It may be fraught with obstacles and opposition. But let me tell you something even more profound - the most audacious dreams often face the fiercest opposition. It is in these moments that you must summon faith and resilience. Remember, greatness lies not in seeking the approval of the masses but in following the calling of your heart.

I challenge you today to claim your dreams as your own, to treasure them, and to pursue them with unyielding determination. Embrace the discomfort that comes with blazing your own trail. Allow the naysayers to fade into the background as you step boldly into the spotlight of your own destiny.

Remember, you have been entrusted with a dream because you are capable of bringing it to life. Trust in yourself, trust in your higher power, and know that you possess the strength to overcome any obstacle that stands in your way.

One of our biggest allies on the belief bridge is hope. Hope is the catalyst for transformation. Hope is not just a wish or an abstract concept; it is the very essence that propels us toward growth, change, and a brighter future. You can deal with your challenges with a lot more peace when you can see the light at the end of the tunnel. Hope is that light.

Hope plants the seed of possibility in our hearts and minds. It ignites the flame of imagination and vision, enabling us to perceive a reality beyond what exists in the present. When we dare to hope, we open ourselves up to the potential for transformation, both within ourselves and in the world around us.

Hope fuels our dreams, showing us that there is something more significant waiting to be discovered beyond the limitations of our current circumstances. Dr. Martin Luther King Jr. said that "hope is the final refusal to give up."

Hope is not a passive state; it is a call to action. It stirs within us a sense of urgency and compels us to take steps towards the change we seek. If you hold on to hope long enough, faith will kick in. Those with "caterpillar faith" can't always understand us who have "butterfly faith."

We all know that a caterpillar goes through a transformative process to become a butterfly - a journey from crawling on the ground to soaring in the sky. This analogy can be applied to our own lives when it comes to faith.

You see, there are those who follow the path of "Caterpillar Faith." They choose to believe that their circumstances and limitations are fixed and unchangeable. They accept the notion that they are meant to stay in the caterpillar stage forever, never experiencing the true potential and freedom of becoming a butterfly.

Perhaps it is because they have been influenced by a limiting mindset that leaves no room for faith. They allow others to impose limitations upon them and freeze them in the caterpillar stage. They acquiesce and keep themselves trapped, never daring to spread their wings and take flight.

People who possess "butterfly faith" refuse to accept such limitations. They understand that they have the power to transform, to break free from the constraints that society puts on them. They refuse to let others kill their dreams with doubt or fear of looking crazy.

Instead, they harbor an unwavering belief in themselves and their abilities. Yes, butterfly faith may look crazy to a caterpillar. There will always be those who try to convince us that because we are currently in the caterpillar stage, we will forever be confined to it.

But what they fail to understand is that faith doesn't care about the odds. Faith is the driving force that propels us forward, even when the journey seems impossible. It is not limited by age or any external circumstances. It is the fuel that ignites our passion, pushes us to pursue our dreams, and ultimately helps us emerge as the butterflies we are destined to become.

Muhammad Ali famously said, "float like a butterfly, sting like a bee." It was against the odds for him (Cassius Clay, as he was called then) to win the heavyweight championship for the first time against Sonny Liston.

Cassius Clay was an 8–1 underdog. But it didn't matter what the odds were; Clay had butterfly faith, and when the bell rang for the start of the seventh round, Liston stayed in his corner, and all you see was Clay shuffling his feet with his hands raised in victory and saying, "I shook up the world, I shook up the world." Ali said, "I am the greatest. I said that even before I knew I was."

Limiting and negative beliefs are like "bad alternators" on a car that can derail your aspirations and those of any team that you may be a part of. I recall picking up my wife from the airport after she had gotten in on an overnight flight. We intended to head straight home after, but we decided to stop at a grocery store to pick up a few items. After loading the car with groceries, we got in, and the car would not start.

Assuming it was a dead battery, I called AAA battery service, and a technician came to test the battery. Surprisingly, the battery tested fine, according to his device. However, the technician informed us that the problem was with the alternator. I reached out to a mechanic who recommended that I buy a new alternator, and he would install it for us. We purchased the new alternator and had it installed as per his instructions.

With the new alternator in place, we tried starting the car again, hopeful that it would work this time. However, to our frustration, the car still wouldn't start. It turned out that due to the previous alternator's failure, the battery had been completely drained of power. I then went and bought a new battery and had it installed. The car still wouldn't start.

The mechanic surmised that this was because when the battery went out, the car's key was deprogrammed and disconnected from the ignition. To fix the issue, the key had to be reprogrammed so that it could be reconnected with the car. We then had the car towed to a dealership for them to reprogram the key. After the reprogramming process was completed, we were finally able to start the car without any issues.

Reflecting on this experience, I couldn't help but draw a parallel between the importance of personnel selection for a team of any kind and the functioning of a car's operating system. One bad personnel selection who carries influence over others can be like the bad alternator that drains the energy out of the battery. As the battery lost its power, the car's key then became deprogrammed and disconnected from the ignition.

Therefore, it is crucial to carefully select team members who possess not only the necessary skills but also exhibit positive character traits and a cooperative attitude. By doing so, you can avoid the potential pitfalls that can arise from one individual's negative influence and maintain a harmonious, productive team environment. On the other hand, choosing individuals who are skilled, motivated, and aligned with the team's goals can lead to greater success and harmony.

One example of a "bad alternator" is a person who not only is guided by negative narratives but also actively spreads them throughout the team. Their limiting beliefs can permeate the group, leading to a collective sense of resignation and giving up before even attempting to take action. The toxic environment created by this negativity undermines the motivation and confidence of team members, making it difficult for them to overcome challenges and achieve their goals.

As the negative narratives become pervasive, team members can find themselves trapped in a perpetual state of inaction. Instead of proactively pursuing solutions, they become paralyzed by self-doubt and fear of failure. This inaction stifles innovation, hinders progress, and creates a culture of complacency within the team. Moreover, these "bad alternators" actively discourage, undermine, and even sabotage those who are trying to take action, further exacerbating the negative impact on the team.

Carriers of alternative positive narratives must push back against the influence of "bad alternators" with an attitude of proactive action. An example of this pushback against limiting beliefs that lead to perpetual inaction is an attitude of "if we fail, we're going to fail in action. We are not going to fail because of inaction." By fostering a culture of collaboration and resilience, teams can overcome the stifling effects of "bad alternators" and regain their momentum. With the right mindset and cohesive teamwork, teams can overcome the obstacles posed by "bad alternators" to unlock their full potential and stay on the road toward the fulfillment of their mission.

When the beliefs that are in alignment with your brighter future become dominant and are now in the driver's seat, you will have gotten through the belief bridge.

THE SYSTEMS BRIDGE

The next bridge is the system's bridge. You've identified your brighter future, and you have built up your belief in it; now you must create systems and processes to add discipline to your belief. You can create systems in your life that expand your knowledge, skills, and abilities and then plug your expanded capacity into a larger championship system.

I had a great basketball development system during my senior year of high school. My regimen consisted of making 300 shots a day and completing a series of ball-handling drills. The 300 made shots were broken down into six sections of fifty, with each of the six simulating shooting positions and scenarios that I would likely see in a game.

This on-the-court regimen was combined with a weight-lifting and conditioning program that had me in good shape. I led or was among the leaders in points per game in the AA division of high school basketball in Tennessee throughout the entire season. I was named the District MVP and the MVP of the four tournaments that our team played in that season.

I had a system for my development in basketball, but I had little to no system for academics outside of just doing the minimum of not getting a "C" so that my parents would continue to let me participate in the sport. One of the things that I would have done differently when I look back at my middle and high school years is that I would have taken my other talent and ability outside of basketball more seriously. I would have repurposed a lot of that basketball time into my bigger purpose.

My parents bought me an ACT preparation book, and I never opened it. I would spend 3 hours after practice on the court but wouldn't even do 30 minutes of test prep. I walked in to take the test with no preparation. I remember pretty much guessing during the entire "science reasoning" section. The Princeton University basketball staff indicated that if I had gotten a certain score on the ACT, I would have been able to come. Needless to say, I didn't get the score. God took me on a different route, and I ended up at Palm Beach Community College.

No matter how talented you are as an individual, your individual talent will not beat a great system. Michael Jordan was the best individual player in the NBA for several years before he won a championship. He lost multiple years in a row to the Detroit Pistons, who had devised a system called the "Jordan Rules" to defeat him. It wasn't until the Bulls added Coach Phil Jackson, Scottie Pippen, and others that Jordan realized that he had to invest in his teammates and make them better that he started winning championships.

Think about your own goals and what systems you can put in place to reach them. It is important to plug your capacity into a championship system because it takes a system to bring about the systemic change that is needed in our country today. Wherever you are, there is a championship system that you can plug your knowledge, skills, and ability into.

Accelerate in the lane you are in, be outstanding in the system where you are, and let your gift shine in the position you hold. Maximize your circumstances, grow where you are, and show mastery over your current assignments. Be a star in your role. You can operate and excel within a system while also knowing that you are not confined to it.

One of the systems that I have been working with others to develop in South Florida is a tech talent pipeline. In the process of trying to develop this system, I began to notice some issues that I will divide into three areas below:

Infrastructure:

With the advent and advancement of artificial intelligence, it is likely that in the long run, we will need a higher level of skill to break in. A lot of entry-level roles may be in danger. We will need to be able to do more than just execute tasks. We will need a skillset that is broader than knowing a coding language. We will need to go higher than the first level. The first level in software engineering, for example, is that you are given a task, and then you do it. The next level is that you are given a problem, and then you code the tasks.

We should be asking if the infrastructure in our school districts align with these changing dynamics. Is the infrastructure set up to take students to a higher level? There is a need for assessments of what infrastructure needs to be in place in different areas and then concentrate public attention on what must be done to create the necessary infrastructures of opportunity in key areas.

From an infrastructure standpoint, I noticed that most schools that I visited did not have any kind of computer science in them or had a bare minimum level. It is one thing to go on STEM field trips and see some cool experiments, but the effectiveness of this exposure is extremely limited if there is not an infrastructure in place at their school where they can gain the needed skillsets to ultimately participate in the opportunity at a high level.

In Miami, I found that some schools in the inner city were just starting the Microsoft TEALS program, so there was something that we could build upon. Other schools in more suburban parts of the county had computer science classes with a live instructor teaching them every day. So, there was a great disparity in terms of the quality and delivery of the course.

There is a need to bring in needed infrastructure where nothing is pre-existing. After it is put in, qualified people will be needed to maintain it and to keep it going. In the schools that had begun to offer some version of the content, there was very little context for what it was or what one could do with it. This leads me to the second area, inspiration.

Inspiration:

Context generates inspiration. Context is very powerful. It would likely not make sense for someone to repeatedly run sprints, do agility drills, and hoist their body into another person for no reason. It isn't until the context of football and the opportunities that participation in the sport entails that it would make sense for those students who choose to play to engage in it.

The context around football has been infused with value. There are clear models of success, scholarship opportunities to major universities, lucrative professional contracts, elevated social status, and the potential to dramatically change the economic conditions for themselves and their families. These are all aspects that add to the context around the motivation for participation in the sport.

The context of sports and entertainment stardom can inspire extreme levels of practice, perseverance, and production on playing courts and fields. Context addresses the important "for what" question. The meaning that context provides can make a critical difference in tech educational curricula like computer science. Coding programs like Python and JavaScript, or even critical subjects like Algebra, are much less likely to have relevance to students if there is not a value-infused context attached to them.

Exposure to people who are operating at high levels of tech, their lifestyles, and their workplaces is critical to providing context to the content that students are learning. This context gives relevance to curriculum and study that may otherwise seem disconnected.

I believe that there is a need to intentionally build context around computer science education specifically. The utility of tech skillsets like competence in computer programming languages is multidimensional as it is used to build websites and software applications that operate cell phones, thermostats, airplanes, elevators, video games, social media, and so much more. These items were all brought to us in large part by computer scientists and engineers. This is all a part of the tech context. Pretty much everything runs on software nowadays.

There are tech students and professionals in our communities who can inspire Tech Dreams. By highlighting and uplifting those who are making great progress in their career journeys, our communities can develop and nurture the required confidence, knowledge, and skills to motivate others to excel in STEM career pipelines. Tech dreams can be used to accelerate people's ability and motivation to plug into the opportunities, pathways, and programs that educational institutions and other entities are creating.

Door Opening:

There is a need for a "door opening initiative" in partnership with institutions of higher education and industry partners to help create opportunities for students. James Brown said, "I don't need you to give me anything, open up the door and I'll get it myself." We need some intentional doors to be opened for those who have qualified themselves.

Preparing people to walk through the gates of tech opportunity will be to little avail if the gates are locked. After we have people participating and they have been inspired to go through the process and build their capacity, there must be intentional efforts to open the doors of tech employment and entrepreneurship.

It is also imperative to find the right settings for you to get over the Systems Bridge. I recently had the pleasure of meeting one of my former students, who had graduated from Medgar Evers College and embarked on a journey to build a business based on his passion for photography.

As we sat in New York Penn Station, he eagerly showed me his impressive portfolio. He explained to me that while he didn't have the newest and most advanced camera, he discovered that by understanding and adjusting the settings on his current model, he was able to unleash its full potential. This revelation became a turning point for him, taking his craft to the next level.

The significance of this discovery extends beyond the world of photography. It speaks to a larger concept, one that I believe is a key component of the systems trail - finding the right settings for your gift to develop.

In life, we all possess unique talents, abilities, and passions. These gifts are like cameras, waiting to capture extraordinary moments and create remarkable outcomes. However, just like a camera, if we don't understand or adjust the settings to suit our individual needs, our gifts may remain hidden or underutilized.

Finding the right settings for our gifts often requires a great deal of trial and error. It's a journey of exploration, experimentation, and self-discovery. We must be willing to step out of our comfort zones, try new approaches, and embrace failure as an opportunity to learn and grow.

It's easy to be enticed by the allure of the newest and shiniest tools in our respective fields. But we must remember that success often lies in our ability to understand and optimize what we already have. By finding the right settings, we unlock our potential and ignite a transformative process. It is through this process that we bridge the gap between where we are and where we want to be.

So, I encourage you to embark on your own journey of finding the right settings for your gifts to develop. Embrace trial and error, learn from your experiences, and trust in the power of self-discovery. May we all have the courage to adjust our settings, find our true potential, and create a future filled with extraordinary achievements.

As we continue to look into how settings may impact us, it is important to be aware and conscious of how you tend to perform in different environments. When I was in the 7th grade, I started playing AAU basketball in Memphis, Tennessee. It was a lot different than playing where I was raised in rural Martin, Tennessee.

In Martin, they valued a more restricted approach to the game, focusing on dribbling, passing, shooting and the basic fundamentals of basketball. In Memphis, the crowd expected you to not only win but also put on a show. They wanted flair and swagger. However, in

Martin and rural West Tennessee, this style of play was frowned upon. If I brought the Memphis style of play up there, I would be accused of "showing off" or "hot-dogging."

Martin was good for learning the fundamentals of the game at an early age, but as I got older, in order to fit in and conform to the expectations of the Martin environment, I diluted my game. Although I achieved good statistical numbers in high school, my play became more robotic and less creative. As a guard in basketball, creativity is essential if you want to excel at the highest level. Unfortunately, I succumbed to the environmental expectations and restrictions and never truly reached my highest potential in Martin. It was only in Memphis, where I was forced to stretch myself and compete at a level representative of my true capabilities, that I was able to play at a level that warranted a national ranking.

It is important to be aware of the potential impact that an environment may have on you and make the needed adjustments from a mindset standpoint to make sure that you still bring your "A" Game regardless of where you are. When you have a system for developing your ability, and your capacity is plugged into bigger systems, you have gotten over the systems bridge.

THE WINDOWS BRIDGE

The next bridge is the windows bridge. It's not just going to happen for us. Change is not just going to roll in on the wheels of inevitability. We have to take an active role in creating and seizing windows of opportunity.

I'm going to use a public policy change theory to illustrate how we can create windows of opportunity to elevate our individual lives and our society. I'm going to give you some history, not for history's sake but for the purpose of applying some of the methodologies in our present time. Some of you may be thinking there are some societal issues that I am passionate about, but I'm not sure how to best apply my efforts and skillsets.

Political theorist John Kingdon (1984), in his multiple streams theory, posited that when three streams are joined – the problem stream, the politics stream, and the problem stream, when they are coupled together, a policy window is able to open up. The policy window represents an opportunity for certain proposals to be catapulted onto the agenda and seriously considered for passage. Policy windows do not open very frequently and often close quickly when they open.

Many public policy changes happen as a consequence of an open policy window. August 28, 2023, marked the 60th Anniversary of the March on Washington. The first March in 1963 helped to elevate the problem stream. The issues of Jim Crowe segregation—of being locked out of certain industries or neighborhoods or schools— had been in existence for generations. Two hundred fifty thousand people convening on the National Mall dramatized the problem. It helped to elevate the problem stream.

In 1963, John F. Kennedy was the President during that time until he was assassinated in December of that year. Lyndon B. Johnson took over with a supermajority in the Senate. He made the decision to prioritize the passage of civil rights legislation. The political stream was elevated in a way that it hadn't been under Presidents Eisenhower, Truman, Roosevelt, Hoover, Coolidge, Harding, Wilson,

Taft, McKinley, Cleveland, Harrison, Arthur, Garfield, Hayes, Grant, or Johnson.

The elevation of the problem in 1963 by the civil rights movement and Lyndon Johnson's political majority in 1964 was coupled with a strong stream of policies coming from the Education and Labor Committee of the U.S. House of Representatives led by Congressman Adam Clayton Powell.

Powell first proposed what would be known as the "Powell Amendment," which was a proposal that stated that federal funds could not go to entities that practiced discrimination in 1946. For 18 years, it never passed because the window wasn't open. The amendment became Title 6 of the 1964 Civil Rights Act because the window had opened for it to cross the policy trail.

There is a need for people who can work in each of these streams, and we need people who can couple the streams together to pass transformative public policy today. You can activate the three streams in your individual lives to open up windows of opportunity.

The systems bridge that was previously referred to can be a part of the policy stream. A problem that needs to be solved represents the problem stream. The decision maker, gatekeeper, or door opener is the political stream.

Recognize the value of problems in your life. There is a problem that needs to be solved; there is a need – problem stream. You have a solution – policy stream; there is the decisionmaker or decisionmakers – the politics stream. Couple all three, and you have created a window of opportunity.

You have a system. You have a gift. You have a talent. You have a skillset. You have a policy. You now must either create a new opportunity or seize an existing one. We should be asking ourselves. What are we doing to couple the three streams to create windows of opportunity?

I mentioned earlier that I started playing AAU basketball in the 7th grade in Memphis, but I didn't mention how I got down there. I was with my Mom going to a routine doctor's appointment just following the basketball season that year. My pediatrician, Dr. Dale Yates, had happened to hear about how good of a player I had become, and he called his friend in Memphis, Dr. Van Snyder, to tell him about me.

Dr. Snyder coached the best AAU program in the state, the Memphis Bellevue War Eagles, and he invited me to join their practice the next evening. My Mom ended up driving me down there after she got off of work the next day. It was over two hours each way.

Even though I had the talent and had put in the work to improve my skill set, an additional effort was going to have to be made for me to seize and maximize the window of opportunity that had been presented at that moment. We had to make a 5-hour roundtrip for the same opportunity that other kids drove down the street for, but when we got on the court, it didn't matter. I wasn't going to get any extra points for making the drive. We had to do the work without complaint and do whatever it took to get to and maximize the opportunity.

Frederick Douglass said, "We may not get everything we pay for in life, but we sure pay for all we get." It's not owed to you. It's not yours for the having; it's yours for the taking. Opportunity costs: you will have to pay a price to create an opportunity.

In its essence, the concept of opportunity cost refers to the value or benefit that is forgone when choosing one option over another. It emphasizes the idea that every choice comes with a trade-off. When it comes to creating opportunities, individuals must recognize that they will inevitably have to pay a price, whether it's in terms of time, effort, resources, or sacrifices.

Creating opportunities is not a passive endeavor; it requires active engagement and a proactive mindset. People are rarely handed opportunities on a silver platter; rather, they must be actively sought out and pursued. It is essential to view opportunity creation as a journey that demands continuous effort and investment. People must be willing to venture outside their comfort zones, take risks, and embrace challenges.

Investing in personal growth and development is a crucial aspect of seizing opportunities. By continually expanding their knowledge, acquiring new skills, and honing existing talents, individuals can position themselves for success. This may involve enrolling in courses, seeking mentorship, or pursuing additional training. The willingness to learn and adapt is key to staying ahead in a rapidly changing world.

Furthermore, building strong networks and connections are vital to creating opportunities. Collaborating with like-minded individuals, participating in professional communities, and cultivating meaningful relationships can open doors and provide access to valuable resources. Networking not only broadens one's perspective but also enables the exchange of ideas and opportunities for collaboration.

However, it is important to note that creating opportunities comes with its challenges and sacrifices. It may require individuals to step out of their comfort zones, endure periods of uncertainty, or make difficult choices. The road to success is rarely smooth, but those who are willing to pay the price and stay committed often reap the rewards.

THE EXECUTION BRIDGE

The last bridge is the execution bridge. You are living and being guided by beliefs that are in alignment with your purpose; you have put systems in place to develop your ability and have plugged your capacity into a larger championship system. You have seized a window of opportunity and gotten your policy passed — you have the green light. Now, it's all about execution.

With execution, you may need a strong "or else." When I first got out of undergrad, my first job was with T. Rowe Price, a financial investment firm in Tampa. It is a great company, but it was definitely the wrong position for me. I was basically a call center representative for investments. I was on the "horns" all day, and my every move and comment was micromanaged. Again, that role may be great for some people, but it just didn't fit me. When I returned back to go get my Master's Degree and Ph.D., I made being on the horns at T. Rowe Price my "or else." It became a driving force, a motivator to excel in class and to push forward even when faced with big challenges.

My mentality was, "pass this class or else, keep going or else, finish this dissertation or else." I would be trapped in a life where I would have to report to the horns every day for the rest of my life. I had to execute or else!

We all face moments in our lives when we encounter obstacles or feel unmotivated. In those moments, having a strong "or else" can be the difference between giving up and persevering. It can be the catalyst that pushes us to take action, put in the extra effort, and go after our dreams with strong determination. So, I challenge you to find your own "or else." Identify what it is that drives you, what you refuse to settle for, and what you will do whatever it takes to avoid.

As I have looked at the sports model over the last few years, I believe that the biggest difference is in the execution. Whoever has the bigger "why" has the advantage. Imagine a scenario where two individuals are competing against each other. One person is playing for fun or simply to be popular among their friends, while the other feels like their whole existence is on the line. In this case, unless there is a significant talent gap, the latter is likely to emerge victorious. Why? Because their "why" is more powerful, and it drives them to give their all.

When we are presented with an opportunity, it is essential that we approach it with a mindset of commitment and dedication. No matter what the task may be, whether it's a job assignment, a personal goal, or a dream we're chasing, we must execute as if everything we hold dear and all our dreams are at stake.

There is a clear distinction between the mindset of a professional and someone who is merely doing something as a hobby or side activity. The professional understands that every action they take, every decision they make, has an impact on their ultimate goals. They execute with precision, discipline, and a burning desire to succeed.

I encourage you to embrace your "why." Identify the purpose behind your actions, the driving force that compels you to strive for excellence. It could be the desire to provide a better life for your loved ones, to make a positive impact on the world, or to fulfill your own personal aspirations.

Whatever your "why" may be, I implore you to execute with determination and passion. Embrace the mindset of a pro and leave no stone unturned in your pursuit of greatness.

When you get your opportunity, go and execute like everything that you hold dear, and all of your dreams are at stake.

The execution bridge is also about completing the journey. The execution bridge requires you to execute all the way until the end. I remember the time before defending my dissertation for my Ph.D. on January 10, 2014, I was visiting with family out in Los Angeles just after Christmas and got into a discussion with my cousin Derrick, who had gotten a Ph.D. in mechanical engineering years earlier. I told Derrick about my plans to visit Las Vegas for four days before heading to New York and, finally, returning to Florida for the defense.

Derrick immediately sounded the alarm, fully aware of the intensity and challenges that come with a dissertation defense. He admonished me about the need to be prepared to the highest level possible for what lay ahead. I recall his words echoing in my mind, "You have two weeks for the rest of your life." His warning resonated deeply, reminding me of the immense significance of this moment and the gravity of the opportunity before me.

Derrick's wisdom served as a guiding light during those intense weeks of preparation. His reminder of the magnitude of the occasion motivated me to push myself further than ever before. It was a big challenge that I was able to overcome. There has never been a great lesson or a great victory without having to overcome a great challenge. There is no graduation without you passing tests. If you get it without the preparation and the testing, you will not be able to maintain it.

But these tests that life will bring you are not meant to take away your strength. But to reveal it.

The execution bridge is a bridge of pressure. If used the right way, pressure can be a blessing and not a burden. Exposure to pressure builds up your tolerance to operate with excellence under adverse circumstances.

I am reminded of what so many people in our society value very highly – diamonds. Most natural diamonds are formed at very high temperatures and pressure at depths 87 to 120 miles deep in the earth's mantle. Diamonds are brought close to the earth's surface through magma stemming from deep volcanic eruptions. So, what it is that is extremely valuable does not begin to rise until there are eruptions caused by pressure. The pressure makes that which is deemed as valuable rise.

Embrace Your Crucible

I invite you to embrace your crucible. It is within the challenges and trials that we find our greatest opportunities for growth and transformation. Elite performers understand this concept well—they thrive under pressure and excel when the heat is turned up.

To reach the top, elite performers meticulously plan, set and hit hundreds of small goals. They understand that success is not achieved overnight but through a series of deliberate actions taken consistently over time. They use competition as a means to sharpen their skills and continually reinvent themselves to stay ahead of the pack.

It's time for us to learn to love the pressure, for it is the driving force that pushes us to perform better than we ever thought possible. The true measure of leadership is defined in a crisis. It is during these challenging times that we have the opportunity to showcase our ability to find meaning in negative events and learn from even the most trying circumstances.

Just as a crucible was the vessel used by medieval alchemists to turn base metals into gold, the experiences that shape people are crucibles. They are the severe tests or trials that forge us into stronger individuals. You cannot graduate if you cannot pass the test, and extraordinary executers find meaning in and learn from even the most negative events.

Like phoenixes rising from the ashes, they emerge from adversity stronger, more confident, and more committed to their purpose and work. Crucibles are not meant to break our spirit but rather to provide opportunities for reinvention and personal growth.

While it is inevitable that crucibles involve stress, we must learn to own it. The key lies in recognizing that we tend to stress more about things that truly matter to us. Stress is an indicator that the stakes are high and that we care deeply about the outcome. By owning this realization, we can unleash positive motivation, knowing that important things don't always come easy.

Contrary to what you might think, the body's stress response was not designed to harm us. It is an evolutionary mechanism intended to boost our functioning and help us grow to meet the demands we face. The issue lies in how we channel and employ this response. Simply reframing our perception of stress as something that can enhance and improve us can be extremely beneficial. Let us not miss the opportunities that stressful moments provide for learning and growth. Embrace your crucible, for it is through the toughest trials that true leaders are forged.

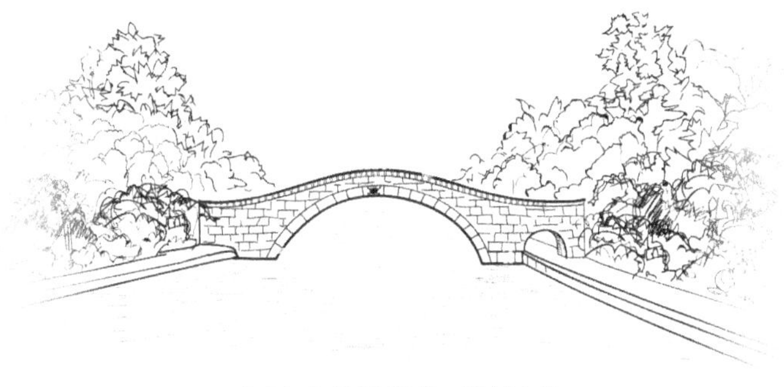

CHAPTER TWO

DISRUPTING THE SCHOOL-TO-PRISON PIPELINE

I recall going to a car dealership because I could hear a roaring sound when I pressed on my brakes. I went to the same dealership where I had purchased my car some time back because when I bought the car, I also bought a warranty that I assumed would cover major repairs. When the representative from the service department came back after inspecting my car, she had a list of recommended repairs that included a major revamp of the car's braking system. She also informed me that the warranty company was not going to be covering any of it because it was classified as "wear and tear."

I said, "OK," and that I would have them do some of the repairs, but I would likely wait or go somewhere else to get the brake repairs done. I typically can go to more of a "Mom and Pop" type of shop to get the more costly work done at a lower price. The representative from the dealership called me back in and said that I would have to sign a waiver saying the car was unsafe to drive because the brakes were "metal to metal."

"Metal to metal" describes brake pads that have worn through all of their friction material. This means that the metal backing of the pad rubs on the rotor, which is also made of metal. Brakes that reach this extreme are not only dangerous but also require extensive repair.

That statement was a game changer for me because there was no way that I was driving off that lot with my four-year-old son in a car that had been deemed unsafe. The statement brought with it "a fierce urgency of now," as Dr. Martin Luther King Jr. famously said and getting the repairs done was no longer an option. I was going to make it happen no matter what.

There are certain conditions in our lives and in our communities that we can no longer wait to change. All of the "padding" or tolerance for this issue has worn out, and it is "metal to metal."

One "metal to metal" issue is the disproportionate arrests of Black youth in communities across the nation. The data is well-documented and deeply alarming. According to a report from The Sentencing Project, "black youth are more than four times as likely to be detained or committed in juvenile facilities as their white peers" (Rovner, 2021, para.1).

When I began working with the Miami-Dade Economic Advocacy Trust (MDEAT) in 2022, I was called in and shown a big packet of arrest data that broke down the demographics and arresting agencies for youth offenders in Miami-Dade County. I was asked to see about the possibility of having a full report done to examine the arrest rates over time.

I then reached out to the Dean of the University of Miami's School of Education and Human Development and asked for her recommendation of the top scholars in this particular area of research. She recommended Dr. Todd Warner and Dr. Mary Avalos and made the connection. I then convened them with members of the MDEAT staff to discuss the possibilities of the kinds of reports that could be done with the data.

We ultimately came to an agreement on the need to commission a report on youth arrest practices and patterns that would analyze data over a number of years. The final report was entitled *Trends in Youth Arrests in Miami-Dade County: 2010-2022*. The data from the report showed tremendous disparities in terms of the percentage of Black youth that were being arrested compared to their portion of the population.

According to the report:

- "The percentage of Black youth arrested is consistently higher and disproportionate to the population of Black youth in Miami-Dade County. While Black youth represent about 17-18% of the 10-17-year-old population in Miami-Dade County, they account for 58% of all youth arrests since 2010 and 63% of arrests in 2022.

- Arrests of Black male youths accounted for 48% of all arrests in Miami-Dade County during the thirteen-year period and 52% of arrests in 2022 despite accounting for only 9% of the 10-17-year-old youth population. Furthermore, in 2022, arrest rates of Black female youth were higher than both White Latinx males and White Non-Latinx males.

- Black youth were much more likely to be arrested and re-arrested compared to White-Latinx and White Non-Latinx youth.

- The pattern of racial disproportionality in arrests was found for all charge types, charge severity, and warrants issues (pick-up orders)." (Warner *et al.*, 2023, p. 7)

The report also cited research from the Office of Juvenile Justice and Delinquency Prevention (OJJDP) that indicates that racial disproportionality in youth arrests is a nationwide problem. According to OJJDP, black youth are 2.4 times more likely to be arrested than their white counterparts and represent 35-40% of cases referred to juvenile court following an arrest, despite constituting only 15-17% of the total youth population in the United States" (Warner *et al.*, 2023, p. 6).

This data shed light on the systemic biases that perpetuate the overcriminalization of Black youth in our society. Traditionally, one would have to wait for a significant development or focusing event to occur, often accompanied by changes in political administrations, to open a policy window. However, in Miami-Dade County, we have the potential to create our own policy window by coupling well-timed proposals with a highly publicized report on youth arrest patterns and practices. By activating the problem stream and illustrating the severity and disproportionality of the issue, we can capture the attention of policymakers likely to be receptive to progressive solutions.

A key component of this effort is the *Trends in Youth Arrests in Miami-Dade County: 2010-2022* report, which serves as a powerful demonstration of the problem, highlighting the major systemic issues that contribute to the pipeline. By providing a data-driven illustration of disparities that have persisted over a decade, the report brings clarity and local relevance to the nomenclature of the school-to-prison pipeline, which may not be self-evident through general descriptions or anecdotal stories alone.

Stories, coupled with data, can be a potent combination when it comes to dramatizing and highlighting a problem. They help stakeholders see the real impact of the school-to-prison pipeline, especially when they can personally relate to the experiences of their own children or other children, they hold dear. The report plays a crucial role in this process, as it provides concrete evidence of the systemic issues at play, making it harder to ignore or dismiss the urgency of change.

The report can act as an important catalyst for policy change, as it provides a benchmark by indicating the percentage of youth arrests. This allows us to monitor progress and assess whether the enacted policy and practice changes are leading to better outcomes. This monitoring is essential in maintaining accountability and ensuring that the desired goals are being achieved.

Developing alternative policies that can serve as solutions to pressing problems then becomes paramount because they can be attached to the emergence of a highlighted problematic situation that has been demonstrated and needs to be addressed. The report is also key because it provides an indicator of the percentage of youth arrests that can be monitored to see if policy and practice changes that are enacted are producing progress toward better outcomes.

Indicators alone are often not sufficient to garner the needed sustained attention for a problem to elevate onto the agenda. Unfortunately, it often takes a crisis or a focusing event of some sort that can serve as a symbol for the priority level of the issue to warrant its placement on the agenda in an expeditious manner. A crisis is what can separate it from the universe of other issues that are competing for prioritized status. In some instances, it may take multiple crises to move it past being considered a fluke and warrant policy action.

Kingdon (1984) points out that categories, comparisons, and values are often employed in defining problems. All three are being used in defining the problems associated with disproportionate youth arrest practices and patterns in Miami-Dade County and how they contribute to the "school-to-prison" pipeline. The report broke down categories of different types of arrests in different locations involving different races and genders. Different aspects of these categories are compared with each other, and different value systems are projected onto people's conceptions of how they feel it should look based on their view and valuation of concepts like equity, fairness, justice, equality, and opportunity.

Kingdon (1984) wrote that "getting people to see new problems or to see old problems in one way rather than another is a major conceptual and political accomplishment. Once a particular problem comes to capture the attention of important people, some whole classes of approaches come into favor, and others fall from grace." Ideas and proposals that emerge in the policy stream do not have to be newly generated ideas or ideas that have not been previously proposed; they can be recombined elements of an offering or a policy prescription that has been rejuvenated and presented again.

It is essential to recognize that these numbers are not isolated incidents but rather part of a systemic pattern that fuels the school-to-prison pipeline. I did go ahead and get all the needed work done for my car's brake system, and I ended up getting two new tires the next day from a tire shop. I did not, however, deal with any of the other items that had been listed as needing to be addressed. This was until a week later when I was getting gas, and my car would not start because the battery had died.

I looked back at the list of needed repairs, and the car's battery was on the list. At that point, I went back to the dealership and got all the recommended services done, including new tires, battery, engine air filter, and oil change. New brakes on a car with a dead battery were not going to work. Similarly, addressing just one of the multidimensional issues that make up the school-to-prison pipeline is needed but insufficient by itself.

This phenomenon goes beyond simple individual acts of law enforcement. It operates within a multi-system and cross-system framework, involving factors such as education, social services, community dynamics, and institutionalized biases. To effectively address this issue, we must acknowledge the complex web of interconnected systems that perpetuate and exacerbate the disproportionate arrests of Black youth.

The consequences of this unjust system are far-reaching. When young individuals are caught in the grips of the criminal justice system at an early age, the trajectory of their lives becomes compromised. Instead of nurturing their potential and providing pathways for success, we are funneling them into a cycle of recidivism and limited opportunities. This not only robs these youth of their future, but it also perpetuates the larger patterns of inequality and mass incarceration.

We now had the report, so the challenge was to use it as an impetus for meaningful change. I scheduled meetings with various stakeholders as the report was being finalized to get additional insight into what some of the best policy recommendations could be.

These included the heads of police departments, police officers, educators, school board numbers, and some of the nation's top scholars on the topic. These meetings helped to give me context into what potential policy changes could be most impactful for Miami-

Dade County and other areas, as this is an issue across the country. By implementing comprehensive reforms across multiple systems, we can redefine the trajectory of our youth's lives, pave the way for a more equitable society, and disrupt the school-to-prison pipeline.

I propose the following policies and strategies to disrupt this pipeline:

Incentivize Trade Certifications in High Schools

By incentivizing schools to offer trade certifications alongside traditional diplomas, students can gain practical skills and industry-recognized credentials, expanding their career readiness. To implement this policy effectively, it is crucial to collaborate with industry stakeholders and develop standardized certification programs. High schools should partner with local businesses, trade unions, and vocational training centers to create relevant curriculum frameworks. These partnerships will ensure that certifications align with current industry demands and are valued by employers. Offering a wide range of trade options, such as construction, automotive, and healthcare, will provide students with diverse choices for their future careers.

Many high school graduates are becoming disenchanted with the concept of pursuing college degrees, primarily due to the rising concerns surrounding student debt and limited job prospects post-graduation. This disillusionment has opened a window of opportunity to redirect focus towards alternative career paths, such as skilled trades, which offer stability, meaningful work, and rewarding financial prospects.

For far too long, blue-collar professionals have been unjustly treated as second-class citizens in the realm of career aspirations. The societal perception of these professions as lower-tier options has led to a misguided devaluation of their importance and potential. It is crucial to debunk this misconception and highlight the immense value and contribution that skilled trades bring to society. By celebrating the skills, craftsmanship, and expertise of tradespeople, we can encourage more individuals to pursue these careers with pride, dignity, and a sense of fulfillment.

The traditional notion that economic mobility is solely linked to a college degree needs to be reevaluated. Skilled trades offer an alternative pathway for individuals to achieve upward mobility, financial stability, and job satisfaction. By fostering a culture that recognizes and rewards the contributions of tradespeople, we can create a more inclusive and equitable society that values all career choices. This shift in perspective will not only benefit the new generation but also lead to a stronger, more robust economy fueled by the diverse talents of its workforce.

Creating new pathways that incorporate skilled trades alongside business acumen is essential for expanding the capacity and potential of workers in these fields. By utilizing existing educational resources more effectively, addressing the declining enrollment in traditional institutions, dispelling the stigma associated with blue-collar professions, and redefining economic mobility, we can empower individuals to pursue meaningful and financially rewarding careers in skilled trades. It is high time we recognize and elevate the status of these noble professions, paving the way for a brighter future for all.

Establish Permanent Criminal Justice Disparities Taskforces

Establishing Criminal Justice Disparities Taskforces in municipalities, counties, and broader metropolitan areas is essential for monitoring and addressing disparities in arrest and incarceration rates. By reviewing data on a regular basis and collaborating with stakeholders, these groups can develop recommendations for improvement. The collective effort would allow for the updating of standards and practices across various jurisdictions, ensuring movement towards equitable treatment throughout the criminal justice system.

Implement Consistent Education and Support for Law Enforcement Officers

The effectiveness of education and support for law enforcement officers has been a subject of debate, with mixed reviews on its impact in reducing biases among law enforcement officers. In order to address this issue, it is imperative to examine and improve the current implementation of such training programs. However, it is equally crucial to emphasize the need for consistent and high-quality training to ensure that officers have the necessary tools to recognize and mitigate their biases.

For example, implicit bias training has faced criticism due to concerns about its effectiveness. One reason for this is the variability in the quality of trainers and training programs. To address this issue, police departments must take responsibility for evaluating the effectiveness of their training programs and making improvements as necessary. If a department feels that the training is not yielding results, it should seek out new trainers who are experienced and qualified in delivering effective implicit bias training.

Consistency is crucial when it comes to implicit bias training. By implementing regular training sessions, law enforcement officers can continuously build on their knowledge and skills in recognizing and addressing biases. Bias is not a one-time event but rather a cognitive process that everyone engages in unconsciously. Therefore, consistent and ongoing training is necessary to create lasting behavioral change.

Law enforcement officers hold significant power and discretion in carrying out their duties. Their decisions directly impact the lives of individuals they encounter. Without an awareness of their biases and the tools to mitigate them, these biases can influence their decision-making, leading to unfair treatment and perpetuation of systemic inequality. Implicit bias training provides officers with the language, concepts, and strategies to recognize and challenge their biases in their day-to-day interactions.

Legislative chambers may draft fair and unbiased policies, but the true implementation of these policies lies in the hands of law enforcement officers who exercise discretion on the streets. Consistent and high-quality implicit bias training equips officers with the necessary skills and knowledge to implement policies without letting their biases influence their actions. It ensures that the intentions behind legislative policies are effectively translated into real-world practice.

By examining and improving the current implementation, enlisting qualified trainers, and emphasizing regular training sessions, we can equip these professionals with the tools to recognize and mitigate their biases. This, in turn, will lead to fair and equitable treatment for all individuals, ensuring that policies are implemented with integrity and that justice prevails in our communities.

Ensure High-Quality Tech Programming in Schools

To reduce vulnerability to criminal behavior and increase the viability of future economic prospects, it is essential to offer high-quality computer science and other tech-oriented programming in schools. Prioritizing access to science, technology, engineering, and mathematics (S.T.E.M.) training and certifications, especially for marginalized communities disproportionately targeted for incarceration, can establish alternative career pathways and break cycles of poverty and crime. Equipping students with valuable skills for well-paying jobs in the tech sector empowers them to navigate towards a positive future.

For example, in South Florida, with the region's burgeoning tech economy and the looming challenges of rising inflation and housing prices, it is vital that we prioritize equipping our youth with the necessary skills to excel in the digital age. There is a pressing need to implement and scale up high-quality computer science programs, ensuring that every student has an opportunity to thrive.

Our school systems are grappling with significant disparities in the availability, quality, and delivery of computer science programming in schools. Many schools lack access to even basic computer science courses, leaving countless students without the foundational knowledge required to compete in the job market. This inequality not only hinders their future economic opportunities but also perpetuates social and economic disparities within our community.

Rapid advancements in technology have transformed the job market, with a growing demand for skilled workers in the tech industry. To ensure that our students are prepared to participate meaningfully in the tech economy, it is imperative that we introduce high-quality computer science courses into every middle and high school curriculum. These courses will equip students with the essential coding, problem-solving, and critical thinking skills needed to thrive in a digitally-driven workforce.

The implementation and scaling up of computer science programs must be treated as a top priority if we are serious about bridging the skills gap. By incorporating robust and comprehensive computer science education at an early stage, we can level the playing field and provide equal opportunities for all students. Moreover, these programs can help bridge the digital divide by encouraging underrepresented groups, such as women and minorities, to pursue careers in the tech industry.

As the tech revolution continues to evolve at an unprecedented pace, we cannot afford to let our youth fall further behind. We must act swiftly and decisively to implement high-quality computer science courses in every middle and high school, offering our students the tools they need to succeed in an increasingly competitive global marketplace. By doing so, we will empower the next generation to thrive in the face of rising inflation, exploding housing prices, and a rapidly changing job market.

The urgent need for high-quality computer science courses is clear. Bridging the inequality gap, preparing students for the tech economy, and closing the skills gap are all compelling reasons to prioritize and scale up these programs without delay. By investing in comprehensive computer science education, we can ensure that every student has the opportunity to gain the skills needed for economic viability and success in our rapidly evolving world. It is time to take action and secure a brighter future for our youth.

Embed Mental Health Counseling into Early Intervention Programming

The proactive deployment of mental health professionals and services within early intervention programming is needed for at-promise students to prevent behaviors that may lead to arrest and entrance into the criminal justice system.

The concept of the school-to-prison pipeline has received growing attention in recent years due to its detrimental effects on at-promise youth. Without proper support and intervention, students exhibiting patterns of poor attendance, behavior, and grades often find themselves trapped in a cycle that eventually leads to arrest and entanglement within the criminal justice system. I believe that a part of the solution involves embedding mental health counseling into early intervention programs.

By identifying and addressing underlying mental health issues in at-promise students, we can effectively prevent behaviors that may lead to involvement in criminal activities. Providing timely and accessible mental health support reduces the likelihood of students resorting to negative coping mechanisms or engaging in illegal activities.

Implementing mental health counseling within early intervention programs will require a substantial allocation of resources from policymakers. This includes an increase in personnel, training, and infrastructure to accommodate the surge in demand for mental health services. Advocating for this allocation is essential, as the benefits far outweigh the costs. Policymakers must recognize the long-term savings that can be achieved by investing in prevention rather than reactive measures, such as incarceration.

By addressing students' mental health needs early on, we can decrease their likelihood of engaging in behaviors that lead to arrest and involvement in the criminal justice system. This reduction in the number of individuals incarcerated translates into substantial financial savings, which can be reallocated towards proactive measures, such as education and community support programs.

Additionally, intervention strategies should address not only academic deficiencies but also emotional well-being, social skills development, and trauma-informed care. By proactively addressing these factors, we can break the cycle of negative outcomes and guide students toward a more positive and successful future.

Embedding mental health counseling into early intervention programming serves as a crucial preventive step toward disrupting the school-to-prison pipeline. It necessitates the commitment of policymakers to allocate resources for personnel and services. By making this investment, we can achieve significant cost savings by preventing behaviors that lead to arrest and involvement in the criminal justice system. Taking a proactive approach to support at-promise students improves their overall well-being and increases their chances of leading successful and fulfilling lives.

Create a Universal Public Option for Early Learning

In the words of Dr. Benjamin E. Mays, former President of Morehouse College, "he who starts behind in the great race of life must forever remain behind or run faster than the man in front." Unfortunately, this sentiment holds true for far too many children who enter Kindergarten already behind their peers in terms of literacy skills, and too many continue to fall further behind by the time they reach the crucial third-grade mark.

Third grade is a pivotal milestone in a child's education. Up until this point, students are typically learning to read, but after the third grade, they are generally expected to be reading to learn. The implications of this educational gap are profound, as it greatly impacts a student's ability to comprehend and master content in the following years of schooling. A publication from the Council of Chief State School Officers entitled "Birth to Grade 3 Indicator Framework: Opportunities to Integrate Early Childhood in ESSA Toolkit" pointed out that "children who can read fluently by third grade are six times more likely to graduate high school on time than those who cannot" (Council of Chief State School Officers, 2017, p. 1).

The significance of third-grade literacy extends beyond academic success. It also has implications for the alarming issue of the school-to-prison pipeline. Students who are academically behind are more likely to experience behavioral issues, which can lead to disciplinary actions and ultimately contribute to their involvement in the criminal justice system. The cycle of consistently struggling academically can also foster a sense of disillusionment and disassociation with the schooling process, which can increase the likelihood of a student dropping out of school, being involved in illegal activities, or engaging in other destructive behaviors.

Disparities that persist at the high school and college level, such as disproportionate arrest rates and underrepresentation in post-secondary education institutions, can often be traced back to the foundational years of a child's education. For these reasons and others, it is time for a strong, universal and publicly funded option to be created for infants through kindergarten to ensure that all children have access to high-quality early education, regardless of their socioeconomic background.

The school-to-prison pipeline cannot be dismantled without addressing the educational disparities that emerge early in a child's life. By recognizing the crucial role of third-grade literacy and the links between academic struggles and behavioral issues, we can begin to target the root causes of this pervasive issue. Band-aid solutions at the high school level are not enough to address the deeper systemic issues that contribute to the school-to-prison pipeline. The connection between youth arrests, mass incarceration, and low literacy rates cannot be ignored. If we truly want to give our youth the support they need and prevent their involvement in the criminal justice system, investing in early learning is essential.

A report entitled "The Economics of Early Childhood Investment" produced by the Obama administration cited research that suggested that "expanding early learning initiatives would provide benefits to society of roughly $8.60 for every $1 spent, about half of which comes from increased earnings for children when they grow up" (Council of Economic Advisers, 2014, p. 3). It is clearly a worthwhile investment that will facilitate cognitive, social, and emotional development, setting up children for success in school and beyond.

The current hodgepodge of early childhood learning options and slots has led to tremendous inequity in the quality and availability of services. The universal nature of the public option would go a long way towards addressing these issues and would remove current income thresholds that too often leave the working and middle-class making just enough money to not qualify for support and not enough money to pay for needed early learning services for their children that would put them on track towards a literacy level that is conducive to them thriving academically for the long run.

The implementation of this expansion of access and quality would also require partners and resources to be corralled to elevate the level of compensation and credentialing for early learning teachers. Collaboration with higher education institutions is crucial to accomplishing these aims. Incentives such as accelerated student loan forgiveness, competitive salaries, and alternative certification programs should be considered to address teacher shortages and attract more educators into the space.

It is time for a revolution in prioritizing, funding, standardizing, and aligning our early learning system. By creating and passing a universal public option for early learning, we can not only help dismantle the school-to-prison pipeline, but we can accelerate the creation of new pipelines of positive opportunity for all children.

Create Non-Police First Responder Programs

The Non-Police First Responder Program Funding Act is proposed to address the growing need for alternative responses to certain public health-related calls that historically have been handled by law enforcement. This legislation aims to authorize the government to allocate adequate funding for a pilot program that deploys teams of social workers, paramedics, and mental health professionals to these calls, promoting more effective and compassionate interventions.

The objectives of this program are multi-fold. Firstly, it seeks to enhance public safety by diverting non-violent public health-related calls away from law enforcement. By providing specialized care and support to individuals in crisis, the program prioritizes de-escalation and appropriate intervention over relying solely on police presence.

Secondly, the program aims to improve community trust in the local government. By demonstrating a commitment to compassionate and equitable response practices, utilizing appropriately trained professionals, and fostering positive relationships between community members and responders, the program seeks to strengthen community trust.

Furthermore, the program seeks to reduce over-policing and unnecessary criminalization of individuals experiencing mental health crises or other public health-related situations. By involving qualified professionals who can provide assessments and interventions, the program aims to redirect individuals to needed resources rather than engaging them in the criminal justice system unnecessarily.

To implement this program effectively, collaboration is essential. Government agencies should work with relevant stakeholders, including mental health professionals, social workers, paramedics, community organizations, and advocacy groups, to design a comprehensive pilot program tailored to the specific needs of the community. Adequate funding should be allocated separately from law enforcement budgets to cover personnel salaries, training programs, equipment, mental health resources, and ongoing evaluation.

Collaboration with existing emergency response services, healthcare facilities, crisis hotlines, and social service agencies is also crucial to ensuring seamless and efficient provision of care. By establishing collaborative partnerships, the program can facilitate the referral of individuals to appropriate long-term support services.

Regular evaluations should be conducted to assess the program's impact on public safety, community trust, and the reduction of over-policing. Data on call outcomes, response times, and client satisfaction should be collected and analyzed to inform potential expansion and improvements. Clear accountability mechanisms should be established to address any issues or concerns raised during the pilot phase.

The Non-Police First Responder Program Funding Act proposes a valuable solution to public health-related calls that could benefit from a non-police response. By properly funding and implementing this pilot program, the government can prioritize the well-being of individuals in need, reduce the burden on law enforcement, and foster stronger community relationships. This policy recommendation serves as a step towards a more equitable, compassionate, and effective public safety model.

Mass incarceration has far-reaching consequences that extend beyond the confines of prison walls. The detrimental effects on individuals' lives and the wider socioeconomic disparities are deeply interwoven, creating a self-reinforcing cycle.

Incarceration has become a significant driver of socioeconomic disparities, particularly impacting marginalized communities. One of the primary ways in which it contributes to inequality is through barriers to economic stability. Having a criminal record often becomes a barrier to re-entering the job market, leaving individuals trapped in a cycle of unemployment and poverty. The disqualification from receiving food stamps further exacerbates the struggle to feed oneself and support a family. These consequences not only hinder personal financial stability but also perpetuate the cycle of impoverishment.

The entanglement of mass incarceration and socioeconomic disparities extends beyond employment in the housing sector. Individuals with a criminal background often face discrimination when seeking housing, making it harder to secure stable and safe living arrangements. This discriminatory practice disproportionately affects black Americans, entrenching the socioeconomic divide. As a result, the risk of homelessness increases, pushing individuals further to the fringes of society.

Another troubling aspect of mass incarceration is its deep-rooted connection to racial disparities and recidivism. The glaring disparity in incarceration rates between black and white Americans highlights the profound influence of systemic racism. The overrepresentation of impoverished black individuals within the criminal justice system is both a cause and consequence of socioeconomic inequality. Laws that limit access to vital resources such as food stamps and public housing for ex-offenders perpetuate the cycle of poverty and hinder successful reintegration into society, leading to higher rates of recidivism.

Moreover, the impact of parental incarceration on children's long-term outcomes cannot be ignored. Children of incarcerated parents often face increased financial strain, emotional trauma, and disruptions to their education. These factors can perpetuate generational cycles of poverty and incarceration, deepening the socioeconomic divide.

To address these entrenched disparities, comprehensive reforms are necessary. First and foremost, there needs to be a shift towards rehabilitation and restorative justice rather than punitive measures. Investing in education and skills training for individuals during their time in prison can help foster successful reintegration into society and reduce recidivism rates. Additionally, removing employment barriers for ex-offenders, such as "ban the box" policies, can provide them with a fair chance to rebuild their lives. By implementing comprehensive reforms across multiple systems, we can redefine the trajectory of our youth's lives, pave the way for a more equitable society, and disrupt the school-to-prison pipeline.

The existence of the school-to-prison pipeline highlights a series of institutional failures that hinder opportunities for success and thriving among students. It is a pressing issue that demands our attention and calls for real system changes. To confront and dismantle this devastating trend, it is crucial to acknowledge the disproportionate impact on marginalized communities, particularly Black students, and advocate for equal justice and supportive environments within our juvenile court systems.

Accountability plays a pivotal role in disrupting the school-to-prison pipeline. To hold everyone involved accountable, from educators to law enforcement personnel, consistent training is necessary to address implicit biases and de-escalation techniques. It is essential to shift the focus from punitive measures to prevention and mentoring, providing students with the tools they need to succeed instead of pushing them toward a path of incarceration.

One alarming consequence of the school-to-prison pipeline is the increased exposure to violence and mistreatment experienced by youth who become incarcerated. This further perpetuates cycles of trauma and hinders their ability to flourish. It is imperative to provide alternatives to juvenile incarceration, such as restorative justice practices, community-based interventions, and wraparound support services, in order to ensure that young individuals have the opportunity to thrive rather than being trapped within a system that perpetuates harm.

Addressing the root causes of the school-to-prison pipeline requires a paradigm shift in how we view and approach education and criminal justice. Instead of relying on deficit narratives that disproportionately target marginalized communities, it is essential to disrupt these narratives and actively challenge the assumptions that fuel them. By designing intentional policies and practices that prioritize equal opportunities, support networks, and resources for all students, we can create an environment where success becomes the norm rather than the exception.

Law enforcement agencies also have a crucial role to play in disrupting the school-to-prison pipeline. Shifting their focus towards responding to violent crime while allowing trained experts to handle non-criminal calls can help reduce unnecessary interactions between police and students. This approach requires changes in law enforcement selection, training, and accountability, ensuring that officers are equipped with the necessary skills to de-escalate situations and prioritize community well-being over punitive measures.

Disrupting the school-to-prison pipeline is a collective effort that encompasses policymakers, educators, law enforcement agencies, community members, and individuals. It necessitates intentional actions, collaboration, and a commitment to transformative change. By prioritizing success, accountability, equal justice, and supportive environments, we can break the cycle of incarceration, foster educational opportunities, and create a brighter future for all students. Let us choose to care and actively pursue the solutions that will shape a more just and equitable society.

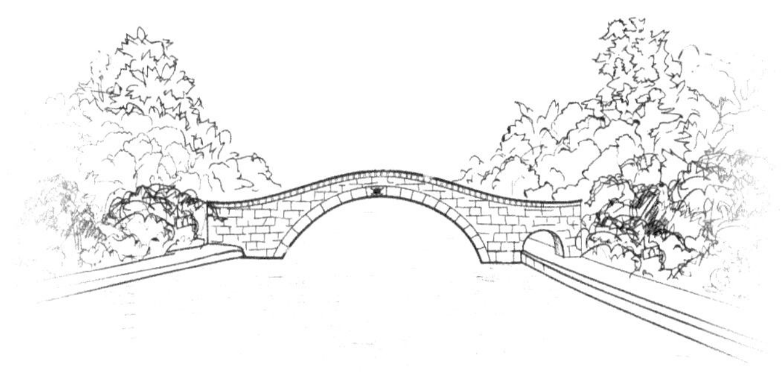

THE FIERCE URGENCY TO ADVANCE ECONOMIC OPPORTUNITY FOR ALL

Dr. Martin Luther King Jr. posed a thought-provoking question that still resonates today: "What does it profit a man to be able to have access to any integrated lunch counter when he doesn't earn enough to take his wife out to dinner? What does it profit a man to have access to the motels of the highways and the hotels of the cities and not earn enough to take a vacation?" These words powerfully underscored the significance of addressing economic issues alongside the fight for racial equality.

The year 1965 served as a stark reminder of the economic challenges faced by marginalized communities. Just five days after the passage of the Voting Rights Act, riots erupted in the Watts section of Los Angeles. This gave further weight to the importance of economic justice, prompting Dr. King to dedicate a significant portion of his final years to combating poverty. He had been in the process of planning a groundbreaking Poor People's Campaign when his life was tragically cut short by assassination.

Today, the issue of economic justice remains pressing in America. Unemployment and underemployment continue to plague many communities, leaving the working poor struggling to make ends meet. It is important to recognize that even seemingly unrelated issues, such as education and health, are intricately tied to the economic status of communities. To adequately address the educational needs of students, we must confront the financial predicament of their parents and foster economic development within their communities.

As we reflect on Dr. King's legacy, we must carry forward his commitment to economic justice. By recognizing the interconnectedness of social and economic disparities, we can work towards creating an equitable society where every individual has equal access to economic opportunities.

There is a need for more bridges to be built between theoretical scholarship and the workers who execute policy and service on the ground. I wanted to put forth a list of policy positions and a model that can be utilized to advance and execute policy so that systems can be institutionalized to help people.

In a world where societal problems seem insurmountable, and change feels elusive, it is crucial to recognize that the status quo cannot be the only path forward. Enormous challenges beset our world, and the solutions we desperately need cannot be found within the confines of partisan politics. It is time for us to rise above the limitations imposed by the labels of Democrat or Republican and come together as problem solvers committed to improving the quality of life for all.

Enough is enough. Many of us are tired of the incessant bickering and political grandstanding. We yearn for real solutions that can deliver tangible benefits to the masses. We crave a new movement that will empower us to open policy windows, creating opportunities for progress and prosperity. It is time to transcend the barriers of political ideology and find common ground.

We must also bridge the divide that separates seemingly divergent viewpoints. It is through dialogue, empathy, and understanding that we can build bridges between polarized perspectives. By seeking out common ground, we can forge alliances that cut across party lines and work towards shared goals.

Believing in a brighter future means not succumbing to apathy or despair. It means recognizing the potential within ourselves and within our communities to create positive change. It means embracing the fierce urgency of now and refusing to wait for others to act. The time for action is upon us.

Together, as problem solvers and advocates for change, we can break free from the partisan shackles that have held us back for too long. We can open policy windows that allow fresh ideas and innovative solutions to flourish. We can build a brighter future for all.

The urgency of our situation demands immediate action. Our communities are struggling under the weight of various issues that have been ignored for far too long. We cannot afford to wait any longer. Change must begin today, and it starts with each one of us.

In the words of Dr. Martin Luther King Jr., "We are now faced with the fact that tomorrow is today. We are confronted with the fierce urgency of now." These words resonate deeply with our shared responsibility to address the pressing problems that impact our society, our neighbors, and ourselves.

But how do we usher in this change? How do we create a brighter future? It begins by embracing a mindset of empowerment. We must reject the notion that our voices don't matter or that our actions cannot make a difference. Each one of us has the power to effect change to bring about meaningful solutions.

By passing and implementing the following seven measures, we can help to open pathways to entrepreneurship, accelerate workforce participation in the tech sector, and advance economic opportunity:

1. Incentivize Partnerships between Post-Secondary Institutions and Employers:

To bridge the gap between education and industry, we must establish partnerships that provide students with real-world work experiences. As industries undergo rapid technological advancements and new demands emerge, post-secondary institutions must equip students with practical skills and experiences to thrive in the modern workforce. By incentivizing partnerships between these institutions and employers, we can foster a skilled and job-ready workforce that drives innovation and sustains economic growth while inspiring students to continue their studies.

Collaborations between post-secondary institutions and employers offer students valuable exposure to real-world work experiences, enhancing their learning beyond what the classroom alone can provide. Applying theoretical knowledge to practical situations provides students with a comprehensive understanding of their chosen fields. They gain insights into the complexities they will encounter in their professional careers, preparing them for the challenges ahead.

Partnerships with employers also help in developing relevant skills, particularly in the tech industry, where innovation and dynamic problem-solving are crucial. By aligning curriculum with the constantly evolving needs of the industry, post-secondary institutions can ensure that students acquire the skills and competencies employers seek. This, in turn, makes students highly desirable candidates upon graduation, with the ability to hit the ground running and make meaningful contributions to their respective industries.

Moreover, these collaborations inspire and motivate students to pursue higher education and continuous learning. When students see the practical application of their studies and interact with professionals in the field, they gain a deeper appreciation for the importance of furthering their education. Through mentoring programs, internships, and cooperative education opportunities facilitated by partnerships, students can see firsthand how their education can lead to meaningful and fulfilling careers.

Incentivizing partnerships between post-secondary institutions and employers also benefits employers themselves. By engaging with educational institutions, employers gain access to a pool of qualified and motivated candidates. They can provide input into curriculum development, ensuring that it aligns with industry needs and remains up-to-date. This collaboration allows employers to cultivate and shape the future workforce, reducing the cost and time associated with training new hires. Additionally, partnerships can lead to research collaborations, fostering innovation and driving economic growth.

To facilitate these partnerships, governments and educational institutions should offer incentives to both parties. Financial support, grants, tax benefits, and recognition programs can encourage employers to actively participate in collaboration initiatives. Similarly, post-secondary institutions can establish structures that promote and facilitate engagement with employers, such as dedicated liaison roles or flexible curriculum frameworks that allow for industry input.

2. Increase Investments in New Industries:

To drive innovation and remain competitive in emerging industries, increased investments in research and development are essential. By focusing on sectors like renewable energy, biotechnology, and the digital economy, we can attract the brightest minds and create new job opportunities. These investments will catalyze technological advancements and spur economic growth.

Increased investments in new industries help attract the most talented people who possess the vision and skills required for groundbreaking innovations. These individuals are drawn to sectors that offer unique challenges and opportunities for growth. By channeling resources into these industries, we create an environment that attracts top talent, fostering a culture of innovation and aspiration.

Investing in new industries drives job creation by establishing innovative companies and expanding existing ones. Sectors like renewable energy, biotechnology, and the digital economy offer immense potential for employment opportunities. As these industries grow, they require a diverse range of skilled professionals, from engineers and researchers to marketers and data analysts. Increased investments in R&D lead to job creation across various skill levels, benefiting both highly specialized professionals and individuals seeking entry-level positions.

By increasing investments in R&D, we provide the necessary resources for technological advancements in new industries. These advancements not only lead to breakthrough products and services but also create a ripple effect of innovation across other sectors. As new industries develop, they often require cutting-edge technologies and research breakthroughs not previously explored. These advancements not only benefit the specific sector but also have the potential to enable progress in related industries, leading to overall economic growth and prosperity.

Furthermore, increased investments in new industries will foster collaboration among various stakeholders. Governments, private enterprises, academic institutions, and nonprofit organizations can come together to support research and development initiatives. This collaboration allows for the sharing of knowledge, expertise, and resources that will accelerate the pace of innovation.

3. Empower the Workforce through Accessible Education and Career Transitioning:

Accessible and high-quality education forms the foundation for equipping individuals with the skills needed for emerging industries. However, many people face barriers when seeking education, such as financial constraints or limited access to educational institutions. To overcome these challenges, it is vital to enhance initiatives that provide affordable or free access to learning resources.

One way to achieve this is by leveraging technology. Online platforms and digital tools have revolutionized education by making learning materials more accessible. Open educational resources (OER) are freely available learning materials that can be accessed by anyone with an internet connection. By promoting the creation and use of OER, we can ensure that individuals have access to a wide range of educational content.

Furthermore, partnerships between educational institutions and industry leaders can help bridge the gap between academia and the job market. Collaborative efforts can result in the development of industry-relevant curricula, internships, and apprenticeships that enable learners to gain practical skills and real-world experience.

In addition to accessible education resources, it is essential to invest in stipends, aid, and support programs for individuals seeking career retraining. Many people may want to transition into new industries but lack the financial means to do so. By providing stipends and financial aid, we can remove this barrier and allow individuals to pursue education and training without worrying about the financial burden.

Moreover, support programs that offer guidance and counseling can help people navigate career transitions successfully. Mentorship programs, career counseling services, and networking opportunities can empower individuals to make informed decisions and connect with industry professionals who can provide guidance and support.

By empowering people to upskill and reskill themselves, we not only fuel personal growth but also drive economic development. A skilled and adaptable workforce is better equipped to meet the demands of emerging industries, leading to increased productivity and innovation. Additionally, accessible education initiatives and career transitioning support programs promote inclusivity, ensuring that individuals from all backgrounds have equal opportunities for success.

4. Prioritize Policies that Support Small Businesses and Entrepreneurs:

Small businesses and entrepreneurs are the backbone of our economy, driving growth, innovation, and job creation. It is essential for policymakers to prioritize implementing policies that support and empower these entities. In this article, we will explore the importance of tax incentives, increased access to capital, and tailored financing options for small businesses, highlighting how these measures contribute to a thriving entrepreneurial ecosystem.

Tax incentives are a powerful tool in encouraging entrepreneurship and supporting the growth of small businesses. By offering tax breaks to entrepreneurs and small business owners, governments can reduce the financial burden and provide an incentive for investment and expansion. These incentives can take various forms, such as tax credits for research and development activities, deductions for startup expenses, or reduced tax rates for small businesses. Implementing such policies alleviates the tax burden on small businesses and fosters an environment where innovative ideas and entrepreneurial ventures can flourish.

Access to sufficient capital is critical for small businesses and entrepreneurs to start and grow their ventures. However, many face challenges in securing funding from traditional sources such as banks, which may have strict lending criteria. To address this issue, policymakers should prioritize initiatives that increase access to capital for small businesses. This can be accomplished by establishing government-backed loan programs, providing guarantees for loans to small businesses, and expanding the availability of microloans and grants. By increasing access to capital, policymakers enable small businesses to pursue opportunities, expand operations, and create more jobs in the process.

In addition to traditional financing options, tailored financing alternatives can play a significant role in supporting small businesses. Policymakers should encourage the development of innovative financing models, such as crowdfunding platforms, peer-to-peer lending networks, and impact investing funds. These alternative financing options allow small businesses to tap into a wider pool of potential investors and lenders, breaking away from the limitations of traditional banking systems. By fostering an ecosystem that encourages these innovative financing models, policymakers enable small businesses to access the capital they need to thrive.

Moreover, policymakers should prioritize initiatives that provide targeted support for underserved communities and underrepresented entrepreneurs. This can be achieved through mentorship programs, business development centers, and training initiatives that equip aspiring entrepreneurs with the necessary skills and knowledge. By addressing the unique challenges faced by these individuals, policymakers promote inclusivity and ensure that all entrepreneurs have an equal opportunity to succeed.

5. Adjust the Federal Poverty Level:

In an era of increasing living costs, it has become imperative to reassess the federal poverty level. Raising the threshold for the federal poverty level is essential to accurately reflect the economic realities faced by individuals and families. The current measurement fails to capture the full impact of increasing costs of living, leaving many struggling to make ends meet despite technically being above the poverty line. By increasing the amount of household income that qualifies as living in poverty, we can better identify those who are truly experiencing financial hardship and provide them with the necessary assistance.

One of the primary reasons for adjusting the federal poverty level is to ensure that individuals and families have access to the necessary resources and support needed to meet their basic needs. Basic necessities such as housing, food, healthcare, and education are becoming increasingly expensive, making it more difficult for low-income households to afford them. By raising the federal poverty level, we can expand the eligibility for social programs and assistance, enabling struggling individuals and families to access vital resources that can improve their quality of life.

Moreover, adjusting the federal poverty level can also help position individuals and families for upward mobility. The current threshold often denies assistance to those who are technically above the poverty line but still face significant financial challenges. By increasing the federal poverty level, we create more opportunities for individuals and families to receive crucial support, such as job training, childcare, and educational opportunities. These resources can enable them to break free from the cycle of poverty and build a sustainable future.

Furthermore, adjusting the federal poverty level takes into account regional differences in living costs. The current measurement is a one-size-fits-all approach that fails to accommodate the significant variations in expenses across different regions. By considering these differences and adjusting the threshold accordingly, we can provide a fairer representation of poverty in different areas, ensuring that assistance is distributed equitably and efficiently.

Critics argue that adjusting the federal poverty level may place an additional burden on government resources. However, the long-term benefits outweigh the initial costs. By addressing the root causes of poverty and providing individuals and families with the necessary support, we can reduce the strain on social services in the long run.

Furthermore, investing in education, skill development, and healthcare for low-income households can lead to increased productivity, economic growth, and reduced income inequality.

6. Empower Historically Underrepresented Populations

Entrepreneurship is a pathway to economic empowerment and independence. However, historically underrepresented populations, such as women, minorities, and other marginalized groups, have faced significant barriers when it comes to accessing capital and resources to start and grow their businesses. In order to promote economic opportunity and empower these individuals, it is crucial to incentivize investment in businesses run by historically underrepresented populations.

The underrepresentation of certain populations in entrepreneurship is not due to a lack of talent or potential but rather the systemic barriers they face. Access to capital has consistently been cited as a major hurdle for aspiring business owners from historically underrepresented backgrounds. By creating financial incentives, we can level the playing field and provide these entrepreneurs with the necessary support to succeed.

Addressing historical disadvantages is a critical step toward promoting equitable opportunities. Historically, women, minorities, and marginalized groups have faced discrimination and limited access to opportunities. As a result, they often lack the same financial resources and networks as their counterparts from more privileged backgrounds. Implementing financial incentives can help mitigate the effects of these historical disadvantages by providing much-needed capital to these underrepresented entrepreneurs.

Investing in businesses run by historically underrepresented populations has the potential to stimulate economic growth and job creation. When these entrepreneurs are given the necessary support, they can create businesses that fill gaps in the market, cater to diverse consumer needs, and drive innovation. This, in turn, leads to job creation and economic development within their communities.

Moreover, when businesses owned by historically underrepresented populations thrive, it has a multiplier effect on the economy. These businesses generate tax revenue, contribute to local supply chains, and increase consumer purchasing power. By incentivizing investment in these businesses, governments can foster inclusive economic growth and improve overall societal well-being.

Several potential financial incentives can be implemented to encourage investment in businesses run by historically underrepresented populations. Tax breaks or reduced tax rates for investors in these businesses can make them more attractive and provide a tangible return on investment. Grants and subsidized loans can also help alleviate the burden of startup costs and access to capital.

In addition to financial incentives, fostering a supportive ecosystem is crucial. This includes providing mentorship programs, networking opportunities, and business development resources tailored to the needs of historically underrepresented entrepreneurs. By combining financial incentives with comprehensive support systems, we can create an environment that nurtures the growth and success of these businesses.

7. Create Healthcare Pools for Small Businesses

Affordable healthcare should be available to all individuals, regardless of the size or nature of their employer. However, small businesses often face challenges in providing comprehensive health insurance coverage to their employees due to limited resources and bargaining power. Creating a healthcare pool specifically designed for small businesses would allow them to access affordable health insurance plans at the same level as large corporations and entities. A healthcare pool that offers affordable health insurance plans for employees of small businesses, enabling them to access quality healthcare without burdensome costs. By pooling together, small businesses can leverage their collective purchasing power to negotiate lower premiums and better coverage options from insurers. This will help reduce costs for both employers and employees, making health insurance more attainable.

A state or federal-level entity would be established to administer the small business healthcare pool. This entity would work with insurance providers to offer a range of health insurance plans that meet the needs of small businesses and their employees. Participation in the healthcare pool would be voluntary for small businesses. They would have the option to opt in and join the pool based on their size and eligibility criteria, ensuring flexibility for businesses with unique circumstances. The healthcare pool would negotiate with insurance providers to secure affordable rates and comprehensive coverage options for participating businesses. By consolidating the purchasing power of multiple small businesses, the pool can achieve better terms and benefits that individual businesses may not be able to negotiate on their own. The state or federal entity overseeing the healthcare pool would provide administrative support, assisting small businesses with enrollment, plan selection, billing, and claims processing. This would reduce the administrative burden on small business owners, allowing them to focus on their core operations.

The healthcare pool for small businesses could be funded through a combination of sources, including:

- **Employer Contributions:** Participating small businesses would contribute a portion of the premiums for their employees' health insurance plans based on their size and affordability.

- **Government Support:** State or federal governments may provide financial assistance or subsidies to support the establishment and maintenance of the healthcare pool, ensuring its long-term sustainability.

- **Insurance Provider Participation Fees:** Insurance providers who participate in the healthcare pool would pay a fee or percentage of premiums to support administrative costs and fund essential services provided by the pool.

THE IMPACT OF ARTIFICIAL INTELLIGENCE AND AUTOMATION

The rapid advancements in artificial intelligence (AI) and automation technologies have revolutionized various industries, leading to increased efficiency and productivity. However, these transformative technologies also raise concerns about job displacement and the widening gap between those who can adapt and participate in this new era.

One of the significant consequences of AI and automation is the automation of systems, which has the potential to replace certain job roles that are clerical and repetitive in nature. Tasks that humans once performed can now be efficiently carried out by AI-powered machines or software. This raises concerns for individuals whose jobs are at risk of being automated. It is essential to acknowledge this shift and proactively prepare workers for the changing job landscape through retraining and reskilling initiatives.

As AI and automation continue to reshape industries, it is crucial to bridge the divide in participation to prevent further exacerbating existing inequalities. Historically marginalized groups, such as low-income individuals and minority communities, often face barriers to accessing education and training opportunities needed to thrive in a technology-driven society. Efforts must be made to provide equal access to resources, training programs, and educational pathways to ensure that no one is left behind in the era of AI and automation.

Governments, educational institutions, and businesses should collaborate to create inclusive ecosystems that foster learning, innovation, and entrepreneurship. This includes promoting STEM (Science, Technology, Engineering, and Mathematics) education, establishing scholarship programs, and providing mentorship opportunities for underrepresented groups. By doing so, we can build a diverse and skilled workforce that is ready to embrace the potential of AI and automation.

While AI and automation can displace certain job roles, they also create new opportunities. As repetitive tasks become automated, there will be an increased demand for people skilled in areas such as data analysis, machine learning, and cybersecurity. It is crucial for individuals to adapt and upskill to remain relevant in the job market.

Furthermore, ethical considerations must be at the forefront as AI and automation continue to evolve. Ensuring transparency, accountability, and fairness in AI algorithms is essential to avoid biased outcomes and discriminatory practices. Ethical guidelines and regulations should be established and enforced to ensure that AI technologies are used responsibly.

BUILDING BRIDGES BETWEEN INDUSTRY NOW AND INDUSTRY OF THE FUTURE

It is crucial to establish a strong connection between industries' current state and their future trajectory. The rapid advancement of automation and the inevitable displacement of jobs necessitate proactive measures to bridge this gap. The current landscape of industries is marked by an increasing reliance on automation. Technological advancements have significantly transformed the way we work, with many jobs at risk of being phased out entirely. However, it is essential to approach this transformation in a strategic and inclusive manner, keeping in mind the long-term sustainability of industries and the well-being of the workforce.

To build an effective bridge, it is paramount to recognize the needs of industries in the present while anticipating the demands of the future. This requires a comprehensive understanding of the evolving technological landscape and its potential impact on various sectors. Industries must adapt and embrace automation where viable, creating opportunities for upskilling and reskilling the workforce to meet the demands of the changing job market.

Public policy plays a pivotal role in shaping industry dynamics and directing their future course. By implementing policies that encourage and incentivize investment in research and development, innovation, and workforce training, governments can help industries navigate the transition towards automation. Tax incentives, grants, and partnerships with educational institutions can facilitate the development of new technologies and ensure a well-prepared workforce.

Furthermore, collaboration between industries is vital for building a bridge that spans across multiple sectors. Sharing best practices, insights, and resources can help accelerate the adoption of automation and drive forward collective progress. By fostering an environment of collaboration instead of competition, industries can collectively shape the future and mitigate the disruptive effects of automation.

Ultimately, building a bridge between the industry today and the industry of the future entails a holistic approach that considers the present needs and future challenges. It requires collaboration, innovation, and a commitment to upskilling the workforce. By embracing automation while safeguarding the well-being of employees, industries can navigate the present with resilience and shape a future that is inclusive and prosperous for all involved.

THE NEED TO PRESERVE DIVERSITY, EQUITY, AND INCLUSION PROGRAMS

Despite the growing recognition of the significance of diversity, equity, and inclusion (DEI) programs, many DEI initiatives face challenges that threaten their effectiveness and longevity. I want to highlight the importance of preserving DEI programs by addressing the concerns and obstacles that hinder their progress.

One pressing issue surrounding DEI programs is the disconnect between graduates and employment opportunities. Many individuals, particularly from underrepresented groups, find themselves struggling to secure meaningful employment. By preserving and expanding DEI initiatives, companies can create more inclusive hiring practices and provide equal opportunities for all graduates to contribute their skills and talents.

Despite the efforts invested in DEI programs, the impact is often not fully reflected in headcount statistics. It is crucial for organizations to prioritize and uphold the values of diversity, equity, and inclusion, not just as an abstract concept but as measurable and tangible outcomes. By holding companies accountable for diverse representation at all levels, we can ensure that DEI initiatives truly make a difference.

DEI programs often face backlash from individuals and groups who reject the principles of inclusivity and equality. It is imperative to stand strong in the face of opposition and maintain a steadfast commitment to DEI. By keeping the pressure on companies and advocating for DEI dashboards, we can counteract the backlash and continue advancing toward a more inclusive society.

Another challenge faced by DEI programs is the lack of financial resources and support. Without adequate funding, these initiatives struggle to implement and sustain effective strategies. By recognizing the economic benefits of diversity and investing in DEI programs, companies can create a culture of belonging and innovation, driving better business outcomes.

Preserving DEI programs goes beyond simply implementing policies. It requires consistent evaluation, adjustment, and improvement. Regular assessments of the effectiveness and impact of DEI initiatives allow companies to identify areas of improvement and make necessary changes. By continually refining these programs, companies can ensure that they remain relevant and impactful in addressing the evolving needs of diverse communities.

Additionally, it is essential to foster collaboration and partnerships among different stakeholders, including businesses, governmental organizations, educational institutions, and community groups. By working together, we can leverage collective expertise and resources to drive systemic change and create a more inclusive society.

Preserving diversity, equity, and inclusion programs is not just a moral imperative but also a strategic necessity. By addressing the challenges that hinder their progress, we can create a more equitable and inclusive society that benefits everyone. It is up to individuals, communities, and companies to commit to preserving and advancing DEI programs.

REPARATIVE JUSTICE

President Joe Biden's expressed commitment to redeeming the soul of America necessitates addressing the deep-seated wounds caused by centuries of racism and injustice. Repairing what has been broken is an essential step towards true redemption as we grapple with the legacy of human slavery and legalized apartheid that has plagued our nation. It is essential to examine the need for reparative justice and the economic, social, and psychological costs of racism that continue to undermine our society. I also want to emphasize the importance of clarity, shared meaning, and active engagement in order to translate recommendations into meaningful legislation.

America's history is marred by the most evil expressions of human slavery and a century of legalized apartheid, leaving lasting scars on our nation's history and collective consciousness. To truly redeem ourselves, it is not enough to simply acknowledge the deep-rooted harm that racism has inflicted on marginalized communities. We must take deliberate action to repair the brokenness caused by systemic racism.

Reparative justice is needed to address the immense damage caused by centuries of racism, both economically and socially. The economic toll of racism cannot be ignored. Generational wealth disparities resulting from systemic discrimination have perpetuated cycles of poverty and limited opportunities for marginalized communities. Studies have shown that racism costs the economy trillions of dollars each year, as talented individuals are hindered from contributing fully due to barriers created by discrimination.

The social costs of racism are equally significant. Racism erodes social cohesion and undermines trust within communities. It creates divisions and perpetuates stereotypes and biases, hindering progress towards a truly inclusive society. The psychological toll of racism cannot be understated either. The constant exposure to racial discrimination and microaggressions takes a severe toll on the mental health and well-being of marginalized individuals, leading to increased rates of depression, anxiety, and other negative health outcomes.

President Biden has the opportunity to take a significant step towards reparative justice by issuing an executive order on H.R. 40. This bill, which calls for the establishment of a commission to study and develop proposals for reparations, would be a transformative moment in acknowledging the debt owed to marginalized communities and taking substantive steps towards restitution.

However, it is not enough to call for reparations without clear guidance and active engagement. We need clarity on what reparations entail and how they can be effectively implemented. The process should involve meaningful dialogue with affected communities and a commitment to addressing the root causes of systemic racism.

CHAPTER FOUR

REFLECTIONS ON PUBLIC POLICY AND ADMINISTRATION

The role of public policy and administration takes on an ever-increasing significance in a country where challenges seem to multiply and complexities deepen. With each passing day, the urgency to address pressing societal issues grows stronger, demanding innovative approaches and bold actions. It is within this context that we turn our attention in this chapter to the potential of public policy and administration as catalysts for positive and lasting transformation.

THE POWER OF INTENTIONALITY AND BREAKING INSTITUTIONALIZED SYSTEMS

Big problems, by their very nature, tend to persist if left unaddressed. They become ingrained in the fabric of society, perpetuating inequality, injustice, and suffering. Whether it is systemic racism, climate change, or economic disparities, these issues cannot be wished away. They require intentional efforts to unravel their complexity and create lasting change.

Ignoring big problems only prolongs their existence. Instead, we must confront them with intentionality. This means acknowledging their existence, understanding their root causes, and actively seeking solutions. Intentionality empowers individuals and communities to take ownership of these problems and work towards meaningful transformation.

Many big problems stem from institutionalized systems that have become deeply embedded in society. These systems, whether in politics, education, or healthcare, perpetuate inequalities and hinder progress. To address these issues effectively, we must dismantle these systems and challenge the status quo. This requires confronting our biases and assumptions and recognizing the ways in which these systems have contributed to the perpetuation of the problem.

Moreover, addressing big problems necessitates a multidimensional approach. It is not enough to focus solely on short-term fixes or superficial changes. Rather, we must engage in comprehensive analysis and action that encompasses all aspects of the problem. This includes considering the social, economic, and environmental dimensions and understanding how they intersect and influence each other.

Engaging with big problems also requires collaboration and collective effort. No single individual or organization can tackle these issues alone. Instead, we must foster partnerships and alliances, drawing on the diverse skills and perspectives of different stakeholders. By working together, we can pool our resources, share expertise, and amplify our impact.

However, breaking institutionalized systems is not without its challenges. Those who benefit from the current system often resist change and are unwilling to relinquish their power and privileges. Overcoming this resistance will require perseverance, resilience, and the ability to galvanize public support. It may involve mobilizing grassroots movements, advocacy campaigns, and social pressure to drive meaningful change.

Moreover, addressing big problems requires a long-term commitment. Real change often takes time, and progress may be gradual. We must be prepared for setbacks and obstacles along the way. Nevertheless, with each step forward, we move closer to a more just and equitable society.

THE POWER OF NARRATIVES IN ADVANCING PUBLIC POLICY

Narratives have the potential to influence policy decisions, guide the design and implementation of systems, and ultimately reshape the trajectory of societies. Narratives possess the ability to connect seemingly distant ideas and areas, acting as a unifying force that mobilizes individuals and institutions toward a shared solution. They create a collective identity and purpose, fostering collaboration and systemic changes that leave a lasting positive impact on society. By harnessing the power of narratives, we can bring together diverse stakeholders and perspectives, forging a new path forward.

By harnessing the power of narratives, we can foster collaboration, promote positive values, and bring about lasting impacts. While narratives have the potential to sway public opinion and guide decision-making, it is important to critically analyze them and consider their biases.

Narratives are powerful tools that shape public discourse, influencing the way policymakers and society perceive certain issues. Understanding these narratives provides valuable insights into decision-makers priorities and the issues that shape public discourse. Compelling narratives have the ability to sway public opinion, guide policy decisions, and shape societal norms and values.

One significant aspect of narratives is their capacity to explain the world, providing explanations of how certain issues are viewed by policymakers and society at large. Understanding these narratives offers valuable insights into the perceptions and priorities of decision-makers, highlighting the salient issues that shape public discourse.

Compelling narratives can sway public opinion, guide decision-making processes, and shape societal norms and values. When narratives align with societal goals and values, they are more likely to gain support and be implemented effectively.

However, it is essential to approach narratives critically and recognize their potential biases. Narratives can be influenced by media representation, political discourse, social movements, and individual perspectives. Thus, comprehensive analysis and evaluation are necessary to ensure a nuanced understanding of the potential impact and implications of the systems being considered.

In some cases, narratives need to be rewritten to challenge existing paradigms and foster systemic change. Other times, entirely new narratives must emerge to address emerging challenges and opportunities. By reshaping narratives, we can redefine our collective aspirations, motivations, and directions, paving the way for meaningful transformation in society.

As we navigate the complexities of societal progress, let us remember that narratives hold immense power. By shaping narratives intentionally, we can forge a narrative ecosystem that supports equitable, inclusive, and sustainable systems, ultimately bringing us closer to a more just and thriving society. Our collective journey toward systemic change begins with the narrative we choose to write and embrace.

An example of someone who effectively utilized narratives to facilitate meaningful social change was Frederick Douglass. During the Civil War, Douglass recognized the power of narratives in shaping the mission and meaning of the war. While some wanted to simply end the war, regardless of whether or not slavery was abolished, Douglass knew that it was crucial to use his pen as a weapon to define the true purpose of the conflict. His ability to harness the power of narratives serves as an inspiring example of how individuals can challenge dominant narratives and inspire lasting social change.

During the Civil War, there were differing opinions on the mission and meaning of the war. While some sought to end the war without addressing the issue of slavery, Douglass understood the necessity of using narratives to define the true purpose of the conflict.

In his speeches, he emphasized the principles involved in the contest and the imperative need to completely eradicate slavery and enfranchise the entire colored population. Douglass warned against settling for hollow peace or prosperity that was not rooted in justice, emphasizing that righteousness alone could elevate a nation. By consistently advocating for justice, Douglass helped reshape the narrative surrounding the Civil War, ultimately pushing for lasting change.

In the realm of political discourse, narratives constantly vie for prominence, seeking to shape policies and influence societal behaviors. The dominant narrative becomes institutionalized, often determining the direction of progress and social change. Douglass's effective use of narratives played a significant role in creating dominant narratives that supported the cause of abolition. Through his writings and speeches, he challenged the prevailing narrative that perpetuated the institution of slavery and its dehumanizing effects. Douglass humanized the enslaved population by sharing his personal experiences, exposing the horrors of slavery, and advocating for their rights and freedoms.

In his speeches during that time, Douglass emphasized the principles involved in the contest, the necessities of both sections of the country, and the requirements of the age. He made it clear that the complete eradication of slavery from American soil and the enfranchisement of the entire colored population was imperative. He warned against settling for hollow and deceitful peace, transient prosperity, or greatness that was not based on justice. According to him, righteousness alone could permanently exalt a nation.

Douglass's usage of narratives played a significant role in bolstering and creating dominant narratives that eventually submerged many competing narratives in the American political conversation. In the battlefield of political discourse, narratives are constantly vying for prominence. The dominant narrative often becomes institutionalized into policy and shapes habitual patterns of behavior.

By consistently advocating for the importance of justice and the end of slavery, Douglass helped reshape the narrative surrounding the Civil War. His words reverberated throughout society, shifting public opinion and pushing for lasting change. His ability to effectively utilize narratives demonstrates the immense power they hold in shaping societal attitudes, policies, and outcomes.

Douglass's impact extended beyond the abolitionist movement. By challenging dominant narratives, he paved the way for discussions on racial equality, citizenship, and civil rights. His narrative strategies influenced subsequent generations of activists and leaders, who used similar tactics to advance the cause of social justice. The power of narratives lies in their ability to create empathy, evoke emotion, and shift collective consciousness. Douglass understood this and harnessed these narrative elements to foster understanding and catalyze change.

Frederick Douglass's impact serves as a reminder of the potential for narratives to inspire, unite, and create lasting social change. By engaging with the power of storytelling and utilizing the written word, individuals can challenge the status quo, challenge dominant narratives, and redefine the collective mission for a more equitable and just society.

Hugh Miller (2012), in his book *Governing Narratives,* highlighted the profound influence of narratives on policymakers' day-to-day meaning systems. These deeply embedded stories guide political and social action, often transcending rational or scientific thought processes. Recognizing the power of narratives, it becomes crucial to create meaningful alternative narratives that challenge existing paradigms and shape policy and practices.

The policy arena is a battleground of competing narratives, where different stories vie for dominance. To advance alternative narratives, it is essential to bridge the belief gap and make them meaningful to individuals and society as a whole. The narratives that hold the most significance are those that people center their lives around, shaping their values and goals. By reexamining existing narratives and creating space for new ones, we can actively break free from the constraints of current narratives and foster positive change.

A key strategy in advancing alternative narratives is crafting compelling stories that highlight the benefits and positive aspects of systemic change. These narratives should resonate with collective values and goals, emphasizing how such changes can address urgent issues and improve people's lives. However, introducing a new narrative or shedding light on an existing one requires addressing potential concerns. It is essential to acknowledge the risks and drawbacks associated with change while offering viable solutions or mitigation measures. This balanced and trustworthy approach ensures that the narrative is embraced by policymakers and society at large.

Embracing alternative narratives requires engaging with diverse stakeholders, including policymakers, experts, and communities affected by the policies in question. By involving these groups in the narrative creation process, we can ensure that the stories speak directly to their experiences, hopes, and aspirations. Creating space for dialogue and understanding allows for the co-creation of narratives that reflect the collective wisdom and values of society.

Moreover, crafting alternative narratives also involves reframing existing narratives to challenge dominant power structures and ideologies. By exposing hidden assumptions and biases, we can dismantle entrenched narratives that perpetuate inequality, injustice, and environmental degradation. Through a critical examination of existing narratives, we can identify opportunities for change and actively shape policy discourse.

We hold the power to transform the status quo through the careful crafting and promotion of alternative narratives. By embracing meaningful change, we can challenge the dominant narratives that often perpetuate systemic issues and instead foster equitable and sustainable policies. Let us recognize the transformative potential of narratives and work together to shape a future guided by alternative narratives that prioritize the well-being and flourishing of individuals and society.

THE INTERPLAY OF NARRATIVE AND SYSTEMS IN ADDRESSING SOCIETAL PROBLEMS

In our quest to confront and overcome the societal problems that hinder progress, it is crucial to recognize the interdependent relationship between narrative and systems. These two elements act in harmony, shaping collective efforts and facilitating transformative change. By understanding and harnessing the power of narrative and systems, we can effectively address and resolve the challenges that plague our society.

Narrative holds immense power in guiding and influencing the actions, beliefs, and values of individuals within a society. It serves as a collective story that shapes our understanding and perception of the world. In the context of addressing societal problems, a compelling and inclusive narrative can provide direction and inspire action towards finding solutions. By uniting diverse perspectives and experiences, narrative empowers communities to work together towards a common goal.

At the same time, systems play a crucial role in providing the structure and framework necessary to tackle societal problems in a comprehensive and holistic manner. They encompass policies, institutions, resources, and processes that are interwoven and interconnected. By adopting a systemic approach, stakeholders can bridge the gaps between fragmented efforts and develop a more coordinated and effective response. Systems thinking enables us to understand the underlying complexities and root causes of societal problems. This paves the way for targeted interventions.

By embracing a combined approach of narrative and systems thinking, we can uncover the underlying complexities of societal problems. This approach recognizes that these problems are not isolated incidents but rather manifestations of interconnected factors. By examining the narrative surrounding these issues and understanding the systems that perpetuate them, we gain a deeper understanding of the root causes and potential solutions.

For example, consider the issue of poverty within a community. A narrative that focuses on individual responsibility and blames those in poverty may perpetuate stigmatization and prevent effective solutions from emerging. However, by reframing the narrative to highlight systemic factors such as socioeconomic disparities, lack of access to education and healthcare, and systemic discrimination, we can drive collective action toward addressing these underlying causes.

Furthermore, a systems approach allows us to identify the various stakeholders involved in perpetuating or addressing the problem. By understanding the complex web of interactions and interdependencies within the system, we can develop interventions that target key leverage points for change. This may involve policy reforms, resource allocation, or community empowerment initiatives aimed at dismantling systemic barriers and creating equitable opportunities.

THE POWER AND IMPACT OF STREET-LEVEL BUREAUCRATS: SHAPING POLICY AT GROUND LEVEL

The influence of street-level bureaucrats on public policy implementation has been widely recognized for decades. These lower-level officials, as described by Michael Lipsky (1980), play a critical role in delivering public services and shaping the outcomes of policies through their everyday encounters with the public. Their decisions and actions have a disproportionate impact on low-income individuals who often rely on public entities for assistance, as they cannot afford goods and services in the private sphere. This section explores the significance of street-level bureaucrats and their discretionary power in policy implementation, using examples such as the humanitarian crisis at the border and instances of negative outcomes resulting from misuse of discretion.

Street-level bureaucrats, including officials from agencies like Immigration and Customs Enforcement (ICE), judges, or local enforcement agencies, wield considerable power in determining outcomes that directly affect individuals seeking public assistance. While they are expected to adhere to state and federal laws, they also exercise their own discretion in interpreting and applying these laws. This discretionary power gives them significant influence and impact the lives of those they serve, particularly marginalized individuals who rely on the public sector for support.

A poignant example illustrating the impact of street-level bureaucrats is evident in the ongoing humanitarian crisis at the border, where undocumented individuals are fleeing their home countries in search of refuge in the United States. Despite the ultimate decision regarding their stay not being made by high-ranking policymakers, street-level bureaucrats, such as immigration officers and asylum judges, play a vital role in determining the fate of these individuals. Their judgments, interpretations of the law, and handling of individual cases can result in vastly different outcomes, leading to either protection and support or deportation and further vulnerability for the affected populations.

However, the discretionary power of street-level bureaucrats is not always used in the best interests of the public or aligned with the intended goals of public policies. Instances of negative outcomes resulting from the misuse of discretion are not uncommon. For example, there have been cases where welfare workers — given the authority to assess eligibility — have wrongly denied benefits to eligible individuals due to personal biases or misunderstandings. This highlights the need for oversight mechanisms and accountability structures to ensure that the power of street-level bureaucrats is used responsibly and in line with policy objectives.

Recognizing the importance of street-level bureaucrats and their impact on policy outcomes, policymakers should focus on providing adequate training and support to these frontline public servants. Investing in continuous professional development, cultural competency training, and ethical decision-making frameworks can help ensure that street-level bureaucrats are equipped to navigate the complexities of their roles and make informed decisions aligned with the values and objectives of the policies they are tasked with implementing.

THE IMPORTANCE OF IMPLEMENTATION: LESSONS FROM JUNETEENTH

Juneteenth serves as a powerful reminder of the crucial role that implementation plays in transforming policies into tangible outcomes. The historical context surrounding the delayed enforcement of President Abraham Lincoln's Emancipation Proclamation in Texas exemplifies the significance of effectively executing policies for societal change.

The arrival of General Gordon Granger and his army of 2,000 Union troops in Galveston, Texas, on June 19, 1865, marked the beginning of the implementation of the Emancipation Proclamation in the state. Shockingly, it took two and a half years for the news of emancipation to reach Texas, leaving an estimated 250,000 enslaved individuals unaware of their freedom. Even after the troops arrived, many slaves continued to work through the harvest season due to the lack of information.

This historical example highlights the importance of timely and effective implementation. It underscores the need for policies to be translated into action promptly to achieve their intended goals. Without proper implementation, even the most well-intentioned policies can fail to make a meaningful impact in people's lives.

Street-level bureaucrats, such as local police officers, prosecutors, and judges, often possess significant discretion in implementing and enforcing laws. Their actions can either contribute to a fair and equitable justice system or perpetuate disparities through racial profiling, brutality, and harassment. Therefore, it is crucial to closely monitor the implementation of policy directives and hold these officials accountable for their actions.

Moreover, effective implementation requires the establishment of reliable mechanisms to disseminate vital information to those who can act upon it. All too often, individuals miss out on important opportunities and services simply because they are unaware of their existence. Intentional efforts must be made to ensure that information reaches the people who need it the most, particularly marginalized and underrepresented communities. This can be achieved through targeted outreach, community engagement, and the use of various communication channels.

Furthermore, a comprehensive approach to implementation should include ongoing evaluation and feedback mechanisms. Regular assessments can help identify potential gaps or barriers in the implementation process and enable policymakers to make necessary adjustments. Additionally, involving stakeholders and communities in the implementation process fosters a sense of ownership and ensures that policies are responsive to the needs and realities of those they seek to serve.

THE LIMITATIONS OF NON-PROFIT ORGANIZATIONS AND THE NEED FOR POLICY TO COMPLEMENT THEIR EFFORTS

I believe in the power of non-profit organizations and understand the invaluable work they do in our society. These organizations have time and again showcased their dedication to making a difference, acting as catalysts for social change in areas such as healthcare, education, poverty alleviation, environmental conservation, and beyond. Their mission-driven approach focuses on the greater good rather than personal gain, resulting in tangible and lasting impacts that benefit individuals, communities, and society as a whole.

However, as we confront the pressing challenges of societal disparities, it has become increasingly evident that relying solely on non-profit organizations is insufficient to create meaningful and lasting change. While these organizations have made significant contributions, they face inherent limitations that restrain their potential impact. One major limitation is the scarcity of resources, including funding, technology, human capital, and infrastructure. These constraints often impede their ability to scale up their initiatives and reach a larger audience, hindering their overall effectiveness.

Non-profit organizations primarily concentrate on addressing "downstream" problems, providing essential support and services to individuals and communities affected by disparities. However, their reach and impact are frequently confined to immediate relief efforts rather than addressing the underlying systemic issues that perpetuate inequality. By solely focusing on downstream problems, we fail to tackle the root causes that continue to fuel and sustain such disparities.

Furthermore, social issues are complex and interconnected, requiring multidimensional solutions that extend beyond the scope of any single organization. Challenges such as poverty and climate change are deeply intertwined, demanding coordinated efforts and cross-sector collaborations that non-profit organizations alone cannot fully achieve. To make a significant and sustainable impact, we must recognize that these issues are deeply rooted in the structures and institutions of our society.

To overcome these limitations and maximize the social impact of non-profit organizations, broader policy changes are necessary. Major policy shifts can provide the resources and practice changes needed to complement the efforts of non-profit organizations and bring about transformative impact on a mass level. Such policies must address the systemic barriers, inequalities, and shortcomings that hinder progress in tackling societal disparities.

By addressing these challenges at a systemic level, we can create an enabling environment that empowers all individuals and organizations, government entities, and non-profit organizations alike, to drive positive change. Policy changes should aim to bridge the gaps in funding, provide the necessary infrastructure and technological support, and foster collaboration among different sectors. Additionally, policies that encourage accountability, transparency, and effectiveness can enhance the overall impact and sustainability of non-profit organizations' work.

It is crucial to recognize that non-profit organizations are essential actors in creating social change. Their dedication and innovation have set examples for others to follow. However, recognizing their inherent limitations and advocating for policy changes to complement their efforts is critical for achieving a more equitable and just society. Together, with effective policies in place, non-profit organizations can continue to amplify their impact and drive transformative change, shaping a brighter future for all.

STRATEGIES FOR SOCIAL IMPACT: TAKING ACTION AND CREATING CHANGE

In order to create a comprehensive and lasting social impact, it is crucial to adopt a strategic approach that goes beyond mere rhetoric and paper plans. It is essential to build an ecosystem that supports and fosters the desired change. This involves collaborating with like-minded individuals, organizations, and communities to form a network of support and resources. By connecting people and ideas, a powerful ecosystem can emerge, fueling collective action and amplifying impact.

Advocacy plays a pivotal role in effecting social change. To advocate effectively, one must be knowledgeable about the issue at hand, understand the power dynamics involved, and possess the determination to drive change. It requires persistence, resilience, and the ability to mobilize others toward a common goal.

True change can only occur when it becomes a priority. It is not enough to simply pay lip service to an issue; action is required. By prioritizing the cause and allocating resources, time, and energy to it, individuals and organizations can demonstrate their commitment and drive real change.

Legislation is a powerful tool for effecting lasting change. By advocating for sustainable legislation that aligns with the desired social impact, individuals and organizations can create a legal framework that supports the advancement of their cause. This involves leveraging existing laws, proposing new ones, and collaborating with policymakers to shape the legal landscape in favor of the desired social outcomes.

Shifting narratives is a crucial strategy for creating social impact. By challenging prevailing narratives and stereotypes, individuals and organizations can reshape public perception and bring attention to important issues. This can be done through storytelling, media campaigns, and strategic messaging that humanize the cause and foster empathy and understanding.

Creating social impact requires a strategic, holistic approach that incorporates collaboration, advocacy, prioritization, legislation, and narrative shifting. By adopting these strategies, individuals and organizations can truly make a difference and drive meaningful change in society.

CHAPTER FIVE

THE SHAPING OF ME

Life is a tapestry intricately woven with threads of personal and professional experiences that shape us. In this chapter, I invite you to explore some of the moments and people that have helped to mold me. These individuals and experiences have served as both catalysts and guides, shaping my character, beliefs, and aspirations. Through times of joy, adversity, and self-reflection, I reveal the lessons learned and the wisdom acquired along the way.

EARLY INFLUENCES

I grew up in the small town of Martin, nestled in the northwest corner of Tennessee, near the Kentucky border. It is a college town, home to the University of Tennessee at Martin, where many members of my community had come to pursue education and career opportunities. Even my own parents, who met while affiliated with the university, were drawn to Martin because of the institution.

Family and community were very influential forces in my life. Growing up, I attended church regularly and cherished the time I spent with my friends and loved ones. Every year, we embarked on trips to visit family in different cities across the southeast region, forging strong connections and building lasting memories. Our annual traditions of gathering at my grandmother's house in Alamo, Tennessee, for Thanksgiving and Christmas further reinforced the importance of family bonds.

But above all, my parents, Phillip and Vanessa Bright, were the most profound influences on my upbringing. They provided tremendous support, stability, and consistency in my life. Their values of service, unselfishness, responsibility, compassion, and loyalty were instilled in me through their words and actions. They taught me the significance of making a positive impact during my time on this planet, fueling my desire to contribute to society and make a difference.

One particular example that left a lasting impression on me was my mother's commitment to recognizing Black History Month. Each February, she adorned the walls of Fuller Street Missionary Baptist Church in Dresden, Tennessee, with pictures and displays dedicated to prominent figures who contributed to the progress of Black people in America. The likes of Frederick Douglass, Harriet Tubman, and Dr. Martin Luther King Jr. were honored, and their stories and accomplishments were shared with reverence. Witnessing my parents' respect for these historical figures and the sacrifices they made ignited a deep appreciation within me and further fueled my sense of purpose and destiny.

Reflecting on my family's history, I recognized the strides my mother's generation had made. My mother, Vanessa Simmons Bright, grew up picking cotton in the rural town of Alamo, Tennessee. Her parents, Burnell Simmons Sr. and Lula Mae Cole Simmons, endured the hardships of sharecropping and tenant farming. As a member of the first generation on my mother's side not to pick cotton, I acknowledge the resilience and sacrifices of those who came before me. Education served as the cornerstone of social mobility for both my parents and grandparents. It was a cherished value in our family.

From an early age, I was immersed in sports and history. Playing various sports taught me the value of teamwork, discipline, and perseverance. I spent countless hours practicing and honing my skills on the basketball court, which became a passion that consumed much of my time and energy.

As I reflect upon my roots and the influences that have shaped me, I am grateful for the opportunities and advantages that I have benefited from compared to previous generations. The lessons learned from my upbringing, the values instilled within me, and the desire to make a meaningful impact have become ingrained in my DNA. They drive me to continue striving for excellence and contributing to the world around me.

THE IMPACT OF ROLE MODELS

My Dad and Mr. Edgar Harrell were significant role models in my life. Growing up, these two individuals played a pivotal role in shaping my understanding of manhood, responsibility, and character. Their presence and influence were instrumental in molding the person I am today.

First and foremost, my dad, a loving and devoted father, was an anchor in my life. He consistently exemplified the qualities of a strong and compassionate man. He taught me the importance of hard work, integrity, and treating others with kindness and respect. As I witnessed him get up every day and go to work, I learned the value of dedication and perseverance. His support and guidance were a constant source of strength, and I am forever grateful for his presence in my life.

Also significant was the impact of Mr. Edgar Harrell, the father of one of my best friends, Justin. Mr. Edgar was a pillar of our community, actively involved in various aspects of our lives. He held leadership positions at Fuller Street Missionary Baptist Church and served as an assistant coach for our Little League Baseball Team. His commitment to enriching the lives of the youth in our community was also evident through his role as the head coach of our Traveling Basketball Team.

Beyond his involvement in community activities, Mr. Edgar displayed a consistent example of what it meant to be a devoted husband and father. His support and love for his family were palpable, and his actions spoke volumes about the importance of nurturing these relationships. Observing his dedication and selflessness taught me lessons that extended far beyond sports or community involvement. It provided me with a blueprint for building strong and lasting relationships founded on love, respect, and loyalty.

The impact of witnessing the consistent presence of my dad and Mr. Edgar cannot be overstated. It was through their examples that I learned the true meaning of manhood - not solely defined by accomplishments or positions of power, but rather by character and integrity. Their influence laid the foundation of my character, instilling in me values that have shaped my life.

As I reflect upon the legacy they have left behind, I am reminded of the responsibility we all have as role models in shaping the lives of those around us. Just as my dad and Mr. Edgar guided me, it is our duty to lead by example, inspiring and empowering others to reach their full potential.

My Mom

The impact of my Mom on me cannot be adequately expressed in words. She was the person that I would call to discuss everything that life threw at me. She nourished, guided, and supported me throughout my life. She was my fiercest defender and staunchest advocate. She was intelligent, compassionate, and a natural comedian. She was an incredible friend, a family organizer, and a meaningful servant of the community.

She transitioned into heaven on January 17, 2021, but I feel her presence with me on a daily basis, even though her physical body is gone. She worked professionally as a teacher and speech therapist for 41 years and emphasized the value of education to her family and all who surrounded her.

She was my Sunday School teacher. She was my life teacher. She always emphasized education at every level of life. She grew up in Crockett County, Tennessee, picking cotton and going to school. She used to tell us the stories of her father bringing them to the fields before the sun came up. They were called "hands," but she used those same hands that picked cotton to pick up a bachelor's degree from the University of Tennessee at Knoxville, to pick up a master's degree for UT Martin, and to pick up and lift the livelihood of generations of people all over West Tennessee.

She picked up faith, picked up hope, picked up love, picked up positivity in the face of any odds and gave it to us. She indeed made the best of any situation. She would find joy during tests and trials and find humor in any predicament. She used faith and optimism to override adversity.

There were countless times when she stood up for me and supported me; she would instinctively know when I needed help. In our last conversation, she was embracing the process that she was going to have to go through to recover from having a stroke. She was preparing her mind for the fight that was ahead. She put goalposts in her head and said things that she wanted to achieve. The stroke left the right side of her body very weak, and she was looking forward to seeing how it would strengthen so that she could hold my son when he was able to come down. What some take for granted can be a fight for others.

She said that she wanted to complete her family history project, and she said that she wanted to write a book about humane treatment in healthcare. She said that "folk ought to be treated in a humane manner".

Mom didn't treat people as disposable. She didn't treat people like they were less than. She didn't look down on folks. She cared about people; she valued people. She saw the humanity in people. She was like the Good Samaritan. She stopped and helped those in need. Took the time to write people words of encouragement. Affirmations of love. Gestures to cheer them up.

Her humor was grounded in love. She taught with love. She cooked with love. She supported with love. She treated people with love. She served with love. Her love filled the room.

She didn't let the environment define her energy. She brought her own positive energy to the environment. She was a bright light who let her light shine even in the darkest of circumstances.

Dad

My Dad is the best man that I know. He has the purest heart and purest intentions of anyone that I have ever met. His dedication as a father is truly remarkable. He was at every game and every function for me, my brother, and my sister growing up unless we had different things going on at the same time.

He continually sacrificed whatever he could to provide us with experiences and opportunities. He is honest, dependable, unselfish, and caring. He has always supported me and put forth tremendous effort in helping me along my journey.

One example that comes to mind is the Equality and Inclusion Games Campaigns across college basketball that I was a part of coordinating. When I needed to be at a University of Memphis basketball game one night, and at Georgia State University the next day, he drove from where he was living in the Nashville area to Memphis and then drove overnight to Atlanta just to help me. There are countless numbers of times when he has done things like that for me and others.

My Brother and Sister

My sister, Marcia, and brother, Marlon, have certainly had a great impact on my life. Marcia always set the standard for us academically, and she was a stellar student throughout her schooling journey that ended up in a Doctorate Degree from Loyola Marymount University. She is very intelligent, driven, and compassionate. She has an empathetic spirit that is concerned with those who are often overlooked. She is a great role model and an example of how a person can both achieve greatly and work to open up doors for other people.

Marlon is a great man. He has always been an overachiever both in school and in his career in the field of aerospace engineering. He is the inspiration behind my drive to create more career pathways for people in the tech sector because I have seen first-hand what it has done for him. More than his professional accolades, he is an even better father who has persisted even in the face of tragedy. I'm really proud of Marlon and Marcia and love them dearly.

Friends

There is a core group of friends that I grew up with in Martin, Tennessee, that are like my brothers: Louis Davis, Justin Harrell, and Haley Simmons. We spent almost every day of our childhood together and continue to communicate regularly. I am grateful for the bond that we have and for the experiences that we have shared.

Phillip DuVentre is a friend who has come through for me time and time again in the clutch. When I was in the process of completing my Ph.D. at FAU, I ended up staying with Phil on several occasions as I was moving through the dissertation process, building Education for a Better America, and teaching part-time at Florida Atlantic University. He was one who I could discuss many of the trials and tribulations of life with and who helped to unpack what was going on and figure out the best way forward.

I met Kaytor Tuan, also known as "Kswiss," at Palm Beach Community College, and he ended up coming to the University of Tampa a year after I transitioned there. We initially connected through discussing the commonalities between Martin, Tennessee and Fayetteville, Georgia, where he had moved to in high school from Queens, New York. It was a real culture shock for him, and we could relate to that social environment. Through the years, he has become a close confidant with whom I can share life strategies and support in different areas.

Brian White has been a friend and mentor to me since I was in middle school, and he was a college student at the University of Tennessee at Martin. I go to "B. White" for counsel before most of my decisions of major consequence, be they personal or professional. Through the decades, he has been a consistent "older brother" who has helped me to navigate life. I have several other friends who have helped to shape my life, and I am eternally grateful to them. I will go more into their impact in a future book.

A VISION OF WHAT IS POSSIBLE

I still vividly recall being in my early middle school years when I attended my cousin Derrick's graduation at Georgia Tech. It was a day filled with anticipation and excitement as our entire family gathered at the basketball arena where the ceremony was held. As I flipped through the program, my heart swelled with pride as I saw Derrick's name, Derrick Brian Coffin, listed under the Ph.D. section. It was a remarkable achievement, and seeing his name listed among the highest academic awardees spoke volumes about his dedication and perseverance.

As the ceremony unfolded, I watched with awe as Derrick confidently walked across the stage to be hooded in front of everyone. The applause and cheers from the audience echoed throughout the arena, and in that moment, I witnessed the culmination of years of hard work and determination. It was an inspiring sight to behold, and

I couldn't help but feel a surge of motivation and belief that anything is possible with dedication and perseverance.

After the graduation ceremony, we gathered in one of the luxury boxes in the football stadium for a private reception in honor of Derrick. The atmosphere was filled with joy and celebration as we indulged in delicious chicken wings and meatballs. Family members and friends took turns delivering heartfelt speeches, praising Derrick's achievements and highlighting his admirable qualities. It was a testament to his character and the impact he had on those around him.

But it wasn't just about the formalities and accolades. Afterward, we made our way to my Aunt Brenda's house, where we came together as a family to play cards, share laughter, and enjoy each other's company. It was a time of fellowship and bonding, cherishing the moments we spent together as we reflected on Derrick's remarkable journey.

The significance of witnessing Derrick graduate with a Ph.D. cannot be understated. It was a powerful reminder that the pursuit of knowledge and the pursuit of our dreams are not mutually exclusive. Derrick's accomplishment reinforced in my mind that with hard work, determination, and unwavering support, anything is possible. His graduation day became a beacon of hope and inspiration, lighting the path for all those who witnessed his success.

BASKETBALL AND BELIEF – AAU BASKETBALL IN MEMPHIS

A tremendous example of the belief and support that my parents had for me was my experience playing AAU basketball in Memphis.

It all started with a routine doctor's appointment with our family pediatrician, Dr. Dale Yates, in South Fulton, TN. This happened during the spring of my seventh-grade year after the basketball season had ended. Little did I know that this appointment would open doors to an incredible opportunity.

Dr. Yates, aware of my early basketball proficiency, made a phone call to his friend, Dr. Van Snyder, a pediatrician and the head coach of the Memphis Bellevue War Eagles 13 and under basketball team. The War Eagles were known as the top youth AAU program in the Memphis area and throughout Tennessee, boasting some of the best young players in the region. At that time, I had never heard of Memphis Bellevue or AAU basketball.

Dr. Yates spoke highly of my skills, convincing Dr. Snyder to extend an invitation for me to join the War Eagles' practice the following night. There was just one small obstacle - the practice was being held at Bellevue Baptist Church, located over two hours away from our home in Martin. Despite the distance, my parents were fully committed to supporting my dreams. I can vividly remember dribbling the basketball on the sidewalk in front of our house in eager anticipation of the practice.

After school, my mom, who worked as a speech therapist, and I embarked on the long journey to Memphis. We arrived at the Bellevue Baptist Church, where the practice was held, ready to give it my all. As we went through basketball drills and began scrimmaging, I found myself playing point guard on offense against a "2-3" zone defense. This defensive structure left me unguarded as the point guard, giving me the opportunity to showcase my skills. I took full advantage of the situation and hit five consecutive three-pointers. It was a remarkable practice that left a lasting impression on my teammates and the coaching staff.

Impressed by my performance, I was invited to join the team for their game that weekend in Munford, TN, a smaller town north of Memphis. Both of my parents made the trip to support me, and I didn't disappoint. In just a few games, I earned the starting point guard position for the rest of the summer, setting the stage for an incredible playing and social experience.

The sacrifices my parents made to provide me with these life-changing opportunities are something I will forever be grateful for. Their selflessness and support were evident in their willingness to give up their resources, time, effort, attention, and energy for someone else. It was a true embodiment of love and dedication, and I am eternally thankful for their belief in me.

THE FULLER STREET MISSIONARY BAPTIST CHURCH TRAINING GROUND

Fuller Street Missionary Baptist Church in Dresden, Tennessee, played a significant role as a training ground and foundational institution in my life. When our family joined the church during my elementary school years, it provided a sense of stability and community that was essential for our spiritual growth.

Under the guidance of Reverend Harold Conner, a retired school principal, university administrator, and a respected figure in the community, Fuller Street Church became a place where I could attend every Sunday and receive spiritual nourishment from the congregation,

Sunday School teachers, deacons, and the pastor himself. It was a space where my faith could flourish.

One of my closest friends, Justin Harrell, also attended Fuller Street Church, and this added to my comfort level. My parents recognized the importance of regular church attendance, and looking back, I am grateful for their insistence. It was in this environment that my faith was nurtured, and I had the opportunity to develop my public speaking skills.

The church provided me with various opportunities to showcase my ability to speak in front of others. From giving reviews of the Sunday School lessons to speaking at different church events, including being the Black History Month Program Speaker during my senior year of high school, I discovered a gift for speaking and connecting with people.

The Black History program opportunity arose when my mom, who was coordinating the event, saw potential in me based on my confident delivery of Sunday School lessons. As my Sunday School teacher at the time, she saw the spark in me and encouraged me to share my gift with the congregation. The experience was transformative, as I not only realized the impact I could have on people but also found my own unique style of bridging history with the present.

Even in later stages of life, when faced with challenges such as completing my Ph.D. or navigating difficult times, I found solace in the songs sung by the deacons during the opening of the service. Our renditions of songs like "We've Come This Far by Faith" and "At the Cross" served as a source of inspiration and strength. The experiences, training, and foundational love I received at Fuller Street Missionary Baptist Church continue to be a guiding force in my life.

The church remains a cherished part of my journey, reminding me of the power of faith, community, and the lessons of history that shape our present and future.

EXTENDED FAMILY SYSTEM

Holidays at Dear's House were a cherished tradition in my family. Every Thanksgiving and Christmas, we would gather at my maternal grandmother's house in Alamo, Tennessee, just an hour away from our home. My grandmother, lovingly referred to as "Dear," was the matriarch of our extended family. She was so loved and respected that all of her five children and their families would make their way to Alamo on most of these holidays, regardless of where they lived in the country.

The atmosphere at Dear's house during these holidays was truly special. It created a tremendous family environment where members from different parts of the country came together, getting to know each other and spending quality time together. It was a time for mentorship conversations to take place and for great meals to be shared. Dear, with her tremendous love and service, would cook massive amounts of food, including her renowned rolls. She would tirelessly cook for days, often being the last one to eat. Her joy came from seeing everyone else eat and enjoy themselves.

The house itself had four bedrooms, which were always sought-after real estate by the adults. Additionally, the couches, two of which could turn into beds, were occupied by adults. As for the children, we would usually sleep in sleeping bags scattered throughout the house, creating a cozy atmosphere of togetherness.

During our time at Dear's house, we would engage in various activities to bond and create lasting memories. Nights were often filled with friendly card games of bid whist while the kids would gather in one of the bedrooms to play video games. We would come together to have meals, pray together, exchange gifts, and take trips to nearby Jackson, Tennessee, to visit the mall and enjoy a meal at the Old Country Store restaurant.

These holiday gatherings at Dear's house not only provided us with joy and happiness but they also strengthened the foundation of love and support within our extended family. We were reminded of the power of togetherness and the importance of maintaining strong family ties. In those moments, surrounded by our loved ones, we felt an unbreakable bond that would carry us through the ups and downs of life.

Looking back on those holidays at Dear's House, I am grateful for the memories that were created and the values that were instilled in us. The love, warmth, and sense of belonging we experienced during those times will forever be a part of who we are as a family.

My Aunts

I grew up spending a lot of time around my Aunts Alpha, Brenda, and Elaine. They were my Mom's sisters and always very close. We would often gather along with their brother and my Uncle Burnell Jr. on holidays, but I would spend periods with each of them individually through both my childhood and adulthood.

My Aunt Alpha lived in Knoxville, Tennessee and has always been a strong source of support and wisdom. She would always come to my games when she was in West Tennessee, and we would stay at her house on our many visits to Knoxville, which was home to the University of Tennessee, where both my Mom and sister Marcia attended. She would make these very thoughtful and elaborate scrapbooks for family members and worked with my mom to accumulate and document a lot of family history that we have.

My Aunt Elaine lived in Memphis and was who I would see most frequently during my childhood. From the time I was 13 years old until I finished high school, I would spend a great deal of my Spring and Summer with her as I played AAU basketball for Memphis-based teams.

She opened up her home to me for practices and games and helped me to integrate into the Memphis ecosystem that included both my friends and her friends. Her unselfishness and willingness to support me and others continue to serve as an inspiration to me.

My Aunt Brenda has been like another mother to me. She provided me with exposure to things and places from a young age that I would have never otherwise been exposed to. She continues to support and encourage me in many endeavors. She is the most relentlessly positive person that I know and has consistently gone above and beyond on my behalf. She is an incredible person and a gift from God, and I am so grateful for her.

HIGH SCHOOL BASKETBALL EXPERIENCE

By the time I reached my freshman year of high school, I was highly touted for my area's standards due to my successful seasons in middle school and playing for the Memphis Bellevue War Eagles AAU Basketball Team. The team consisted of some of the best players in the Memphis area, which has long been known for producing stellar basketball prospects.

I was excited about being a starter from my first game as a freshman in high school, but that excitement soon turned into a reality check. Our team was not very good. We started on a losing streak of 8 or 9 games, and the team morale was low. It was an early glimpse into how people handle failure and adversity. Some teammates had a perpetually bad attitude, some turned on each other, some became disillusioned, some kept their poise, and others started focusing solely on individual numbers. It was a learning experience for me because it was the first time that I had experienced such consistent loss. Up until then, my teams had always been undefeated or nearly undefeated.

I broke a bone in my foot during a Christmas Tournament during my junior year. This big setback forced me to miss the remainder of the season and I found myself in a non-weight-bearing cast for nearly three months. During my recovery, I faced an unexpected challenge — my eating habits. Without the daily workouts and basketball practices, I gained close to 30 pounds. As a point guard, speed, agility, and quickness are essential, but with the weight gain, I felt more like a football linebacker than a basketball player.

The weight gain added to my anxiety about missing out on opportunities. At the time of my injury, my numbers on the court were as good as any of the Tennessee "Mr. Basketball" finalists in my division. I felt like I had let a golden opportunity slip through my fingers, and it seemed like my chances of realizing my basketball dreams were slipping away.

Living in rural Martin, Tennessee, my exposure to college basketball coaches largely came through playing AAU basketball for the Memphis Y.O.M.C.A. This renowned program, heavily sponsored by Nike, had produced talented players and consistently churned out Division I prospects.

My previous two summers playing for the Y.O.M.C.A had earned me national rankings and recognition like being named as a high honorable mention All-American by Street & Smith Magazine. I was poised for a breakthrough, but my injury had left me in a compromised position.

Just as my high school season ended and the summer AAU season was about to begin, I was cleared to exercise. However, I was still 25 pounds overweight and out of shape. Despite knowing that I wasn't fully ready, I rushed myself back onto the court to practice with the Y.O.M.C.A team at the Finch Center on the University of Memphis campus.

My performance during that time was lackluster, and I found myself coming off the bench instead of being in the starting lineup. My skills were rusty, and I felt slow and out of place. It was a humbling experience that shook my confidence like never before.

To compound matters, when the team headed to Orlando for the AAU National Championships, I was left behind. I went from being one of the top players in Tennessee to not even making the trip. One missed opportunity had shifted the trajectory of my basketball career.

Realizing the gravity of the situation, I learned a valuable lesson about seizing opportunities. I understood that it's better to wait until you are fully prepared to perform at a high level rather than rushing and squandering critical chances that may never come again. This experience motivated me to embark on a strict conditioning regimen that Fall that I combined with dedicated daily practice of my skills.

As my senior season approached, I was determined to make a statement. In scrimmages, I averaged over 40 points per game. The momentum carried into the first game of the season when I scored 42 points and hit a buzzer-beating game-winning shot against Lexington.

I made the mistake of allowing myself to relax when the football players returned after their run to the state championship game, diminishing the sense of urgency that had driven me during the early portion of the season. By taking my foot off the gas, both physically and mentally, I was setting myself up for a decline in performance.

While my scoring numbers remained impressive, leading Class AA in the state of Tennessee, I couldn't shake the nagging feeling that it could have been so much more. We squandered the chance for a historic season, both individually and for the team.

Ultimately, I had a great overall experience growing up playing basketball. I began playing at a very young age, and it became more than just a sport to me; it became a way of life. It served as an escape, occupying the majority of my free time until I left Martin at the age of 18. It taught me the importance of practice and persistence and it showed me that hard work could yield tangible results on the court.

Basketball was celebrated in our community. It was elevated and valued in a way that nothing else was outside of football. Society and the people in my town placed great importance on sports, providing me with external motivation to pursue my basketball aspirations. From an early age, I recognized that the game of basketball could open doors and create opportunities, potentially leading me to college and even a career in the professional ranks.

Through basketball, I learned valuable life lessons. Playing with others taught me the importance of teamwork and collaboration. Overcoming adversity on the court translated into resilience and determination off the court. I developed the ability to self-assess and identify weaknesses in my game, highlighting the importance of continuous improvement. These lessons extended beyond the basketball court and helped to shape my character and prepare me for success in other areas of life.

The mental and physical preparation required to achieve success in basketball can be applied to any endeavor. The discipline, focus, and perseverance cultivated through the sport are transferable traits that can bring value for years to come, long after one's formal years of playing competitive athletics have passed. Unfortunately, not everyone recognizes the potential of these skills to positively impact their lives outside of sports.

Basketball was more than just a game for me. It was a journey of personal growth and self-discovery. It taught me the value of hard work, persistence, and continuous improvement. Through basketball, I discovered my own strengths and weaknesses, and I learned how to leverage them to achieve success. As I look back on my basketball career, I am grateful for the opportunities it provided and the lessons it imparted.

PALM BEACH COMMUNITY COLLEGE

After my senior season in high school, I was faced with the question of where I would go next. From the summer leading into my junior year, I had been receiving tons of letters from college basketball programs across the country. I remember getting my first letter from Louisiana State University (LSU) as a freshman in high school.

There were some things, however, about the recruitment process that I did not fully grasp. For one, letters and even phone calls are not actual scholarship offers. Secondly, most programs were only going to sign one player at my position in their entire recruiting class.

When my foot injury during my junior season sidelined me from playing in the big AAU showcase tournaments that summer, I missed a key window of opportunity when the nation's top players in my position were being evaluated and offered scholarships.

There were some schools that had expressed interest previously and informed me that they had already signed their point guard for my class. As my season concluded, I found myself with just a few scholarship offers. At that point, I began to think about the junior college option, something that I had not previously considered.

I chose to go to Palm Beach Community College (PBCC) because I liked its South Florida location, the weather, the diverse population, and the chance to potentially play at a higher level of college basketball after leaving there.

I arrived in August of 2002, not knowing anyone in the state. My scholarship covered my tuition, books, and housing. The issue was that it did not cover food, and there was only a cafeteria on the campus that was open during the day that some other players had "meal tickets" and could eat at.

We all lived off campus in a place called the Student Village. Trying to figure out how and what I was going to eat was a struggle throughout the entirety of my two years there. My parents would send me some money, and my grandmother "Dear" would also, but that money really had to stretch in order for me to survive, and I figured out how to live as a minimalist.

My diet mainly consisted of packages of turkey franks, peanut butter sandwiches, grilled cheese sandwiches, $1.00 Totino's pizzas, and oatmeal. It was through that experience that I developed a super tolerance for risks because I know that I can live long periods of time with very little money as long as I have shelter and a place to sleep.

The teams during both of my years at PBCC were really talented, with several players who had both transferred in from NCAA Division I programs and would go on to play at quality programs. The competition was intense every day, and we were all vying for playing time to win as a team on the court and garner another scholarship to compete on a higher level and continue our higher education journey.

In a crowded backcourt both years, I was able to find a niche as a three-point specialist and eventually a lockdown defender. The focus on defense was new for me, and I mostly concerned myself with scoring in high school.

In college, however, I played alongside great players who were also ball-dominant. I had to find other ways to add value, distinguish myself, and earn a starting role. We eventually made a run into the state tournament my sophomore year, but the bulk of my development came off the court.

The classes were not super challenging, and outside of basketball practice, I had a lot of free time. I used that time to ride my bike across the area and to do a ton of reading. I dove into Black history books and self-development books of all kinds and grew a lot intellectually and mentally during that time.

Despite my struggles to eat at times, I was very appreciative to be in South Florida and to have an opportunity to play college basketball and compete with some talented guys. I will always be thankful to my coaches there, Steve Bernath and Brian Mullican, for the opportunity.

UNIVERSITY OF TAMPA

By the end of my time at PBCC, I had really fallen in love with South Florida and wanted to stay somewhere nearby to continue my career and education. Location was my top priority in deciding where to go next.

The University of Tampa (UT) was recruiting me, and after my visit there, I was sold. It was like a hidden gem, a gorgeous campus with several modern buildings located right next to Tampa's downtown. It was near the Channelside and Ybor City entertainment districts, and the campus environment was incredible.

After playing pickup games with the team on my visit and going to one of the coaches' houses for a cookout, I sensed that it was a positive environment. Coach Richard Schmidt offered me a full scholarship the next morning at breakfast, and I gladly accepted.

I enjoyed my time at UT; the housing arrangements were great, I had access to a great cafeteria, and I was able to take some interesting classes in my Government and World Affairs major. My individual performance on the court and the team's performance was average, but by that time, I already had a full understanding of basketball's role as a vehicle to pay for my undergraduate education and a way to stay in Florida, and I was grateful.

GOING TO FIU

After failing to get a long-term professional basketball contract after a short sting in Argentina, I decided to return to school to pursue a master's degree in public administration at Florida International University (FIU) in Miami. I moved in with my brother Marlon, who was in his third year at FIU. The circumstances were far from ideal, as we only had one key that couldn't be duplicated. To ensure we didn't lock ourselves out, we resorted to leaving the door unlocked and hiding the key beneath the exterior window seal. It was a makeshift solution that worked for a while, but unfortunately, it didn't go unnoticed by others. One fateful day, our apartment was broken into, and Marlon's computer and other valuable devices were stolen. The incident shook us both, highlighting the vulnerability and unpredictability of our living situation.

Despite the challenges we faced, I will always be grateful for my brother's generosity in allowing me to stay with him. Our cramped living quarters may not have been ideal, but it gave us an opportunity to reconnect and spend quality time together that had been lacking in recent years. As I observed Marlon's work ethic and study habits, I gained a newfound appreciation for his determination and resilience. Balancing the demands of being a computer engineering major and a member of the men's basketball team was no easy feat, yet he managed to excel in both domains. I vividly remember him rushing straight from a late-night game to the engineering lab, where he would diligently study until the wee hours of the morning.

During this period, one person emerged as a guiding light for both Marlon and me—Dr. Rosa Jones. Dr. Jones played a pivotal role in Marlon's life, recruiting him as a scholar during his high school days at Westview High School in Martin, TN. She recognized his potential and went above and beyond to arrange his academic recruiting visit, an opportunity typically reserved for standout athletes. Throughout Marlon's time at FIU, Dr. Jones continued to support him, directing him toward valuable resources and opportunities that would further his growth and success.

Dr. Jones extended her guidance and support to me as well. Thanks to her influence, I was fortunate enough to secure a position as a student-athlete academic coordinator at FIU. Her dedication and belief in our potential inspired us both. She wielded her intelligence, compassion, and positional power to create opportunities that would have otherwise been unattainable. Dr. Rosa Jones became an indelible part of our journey, embodying the transformative impact that passionate educators can have on the lives of their students.

As a student-athlete academic coordinator at FIU, my role was to support and guide the athletes in balancing their athletic commitments with their academic responsibilities. Assigned to a large portion of the football team, including the entire freshman class, as well as the men's basketball team, I quickly realized that many of these student-athletes were facing significant academic struggles.

It became evident that these young athletes possessed the will and determination to succeed, but they were not always the most academically equipped for the challenges of a traditional university environment. This realization not only sparked my concern for their individual success but also ignited a deeper curiosity about the state of K-12 schools and the thousands of students who did not receive athletic scholarships.

To gain a better understanding of the education system's impact on these young athletes' academic preparedness, I embarked on a journey to investigate the issues at hand. One pivotal moment came when I attended a Miami Northwestern Senior High School football game at the Orange Bowl stadium. The electrifying atmosphere and the undeniable skill exhibited by the players on the field were awe-inspiring. However, it also raised questions about the educational opportunities available to these talented student-athletes beyond the realm of sports.

This eye-opening experience served as a catalyst for me to delve deeper into the intricate relationship between sports and academics. I recognized that sports, particularly football and basketball, had become focal points for urban communities, providing a pathway to upward mobility. However, I couldn't help but wonder how we could extend this opportunity to all students, not just those gifted with athletic talent.

Motivated by this newfound purpose, I began researching the development infrastructure surrounding football and basketball in urban America. I delved into studies, interviewed educators, and examined programs that addressed the academic needs of student-athletes. My goal was to find ways to bridge the gap between sports and academics, ultimately advancing socioeconomic mobility for students in underserved communities.

Through my exploration, I discovered the importance of comprehensive support systems, mentorship programs, and academic resources tailored specifically to student-athletes. I became an advocate for implementing these strategies not just at FIU but also within K-12 schools. By forging stronger connections between athletics and academics, we could create a more equitable system that expands opportunities for all students, regardless of their athletic abilities.

My journey to understand the condition of K-12 schools and the impact of athletics on academic preparedness had transformed into a mission to effect positive change. I was determined to break down the barriers that hindered the educational success of young athletes and pave the way for a brighter future.

HUFFINGTON POST

In the Fall of 2011, in an effort to get more plugged into the political scene in Florida, I attended a Democratic Party Conference of some sort in Orlando. I have forgotten what the impetus was for me to go, but I remember meeting a man who gave a passionate speech about the plight of those who had been formerly convicted of a felony in the state of Florida.

That man's name was Desmond Meade. He had formerly served time in prison and was one of the formerly convicted persons who were being denied many rights, including the right to vote. We formed a friendship in part because we were in close proximity as I was working as a student-athlete academic coordinator at FIU, and he was a student at the FIU Law School.

Desmond would go on to be a primary catalyst for the pushing and passage of Amendment 4 in 2018, which restored the voting rights of most of those who had been formerly convicted of a felony in Florida.

As a part of his advocacy efforts, he would publish pieces from time to time in the Huffington Post. I didn't have a second thought about that until then Head Basketball Coach Isiah Thomas was fired. I took offense at the manner in which it was done and with the characterization of Thomas by some members of the national media.

I wrote a response op-ed entitled "The Isiah Thomas That I Know," and Desmond helped me to get it published in the Huffington

Post. I would submit a few more articles for publication before I ultimately became a regular contributor, publishing nearly 100 pieces. Writing for the Huffington Post proved to be an invaluable stepping stone in my writing career. It provided me with a dynamic platform to share my perspectives, challenge conventional narratives, and spark conversations on pressing societal problems. My initial forays into submitting articles for publication were met with growing success, further fueling my determination to make a lasting impact through the power of the written word.

As I became more entrenched in the world of journalism and advocacy, my experiences with the Huffington Post revealed the untapped potential within me to contribute meaningfully to the discourse surrounding crucial issues. Each article I crafted was an opportunity to shed light on injustices, highlight innovative solutions, and catalyze change. The process of researching and writing deepened my understanding of complex problems and compelled me to amplify voices often marginalized or overlooked.

Driven by a desire to make a sustained impact, I continued to submit articles to the Huffington Post. With each acceptance, my confidence grew, fueling my passion for writing and activism. Eventually, I was offered the opportunity to become a regular contributor, entailing the responsibility of publishing thought-provoking content on a consistent basis.

Being a regular contributor allowed me to engage with a broader audience and truly make a difference. I tackled topics ranging from social inequality and environmental degradation to education reform and healthcare access. The feedback I received from readers was overwhelmingly positive, indicating that my words were resonating and inspiring others to take action.

The Huffington Post not only amplified my voice but also connected me with a network of like-minded individuals who were equally committed to driving positive change. Collaborative endeavors emerged, leading to partnerships with influential organizations and the opportunity to participate in impactful initiatives.

EDUCATION FOR A BETTER AMERICA

During the summer of 2012, I had the privilege of being a part of a small group that transformed the non-profit organization Education for a Better America (EBA) from a mere concept on paper into an organization that facilitated educational programs in several cities across the country. EBA was established with the purpose of creating an educational system that would cater to the needs of students in urban communities. Our aim was to bridge the gap between policymakers and the classroom by supporting innovative approaches to education, fostering dialogue among policymakers, community leaders, educators, parents, and students, and disseminating information that would positively impact our schools.

When we first started, we had no staff and very limited funding, with only a small grant from Coca-Cola. However, we were driven by a shared vision to address the underrepresentation of low-income students in colleges and universities. Despite their academic qualifications, these students faced significant barriers to enrollment and success in higher education.

Our initial initiative focused on increasing awareness about the college-going process and preventing dropouts. We launched a higher education awareness and dropout prevention program, which aimed to encourage post-secondary education, promote civic engagement, prevent school dropouts, enhance financial literacy, and promote overall health and wellness nationwide.

In October 2012, our initiative kicked off at Florida Memorial University, where we conducted sessions on college selection, admissions processes, exam preparation, pre-college programs, scholarships, financial aid, and college readiness. We also organized a youth town hall, bringing together policymakers from across South Florida to engage with the students.

Partnering with Florida International University (FIU) and Miami-Dade County Public Schools (MDCPS) in the Spring of 2013, we expanded our initiative to reach over 700 students from 21 different schools. Through workshops on college admissions, financial aid, health and wellness, and a campus tour, we provided valuable resources and support to these students.

Recognizing the crisis in Philadelphia's school district at the beginning of the 2013-2014 school year, where budget deficits and layoffs were threatening the education system, we brought our initiative to the city. Workshop sessions on college and career readiness, health and wellness, and understanding the Patient Protection and Affordable Care Act were conducted, and influential figures such as Philadelphia Mayor Michael Nutter and School District Superintendent Dr. William Hite delivered remarks.

The situation in Philadelphia highlighted the need for urgent action to address the funding crisis in public education across the country. We emphasized the necessity for a comprehensive funding plan that prioritizes the needs of Philadelphia's schools and students. The city's children should not have had to bear the burden of surviving on limited resources; instead, the focus should have been on closing the achievement gap, ensuring college and career readiness, and tackling the dropout crisis.

We expanded our initiatives to Fort Myers, FL, Hempstead, NY, and Atlanta, GA, striving to impact urban areas where educational challenges were prevalent. In 2014, we conducted a Higher Education Awareness Tour across Miami-Dade County, reaching 17 public high schools with assemblies on college readiness and voter registration.

In addition to our Higher Education Awareness Initiative, we also launched a Health and Wellness Initiative in December 2012. This involved hosting free exercise classes at the National Action Network headquarters in Harlem, NY and organizing health and wellness forums where experts addressed major health challenges, distributed nutrition literature and provided health screenings.

Our efforts garnered significant attention and support. In January 2013, we hosted a Martin Luther King Day Luncheon in Washington, D.C., featuring speakers such as U.S. Secretary of Education Arne Duncan, U.S. Secretary of Health and Human Services Kathleen Sebelius, and Martin Luther King III.

Partnering with the New York City Department of Education, we extended our Health and Wellness Initiative to public schools in Brooklyn and Manhattan. These assemblies focused on nutrition, healthy lifestyles, and education, providing valuable information to both students and parents.

Collaborating with the National Action Network, we organized a Health Care Awards Luncheon in Washington, D.C., honoring leaders in the field. This event aimed to raise awareness about healthcare issues and inspire positive change. Valerie Jarrett, White House Senior Adviser, delivered the keynote address.

Expanding our initiatives, we launched the Sports and Academics Initiative in Detroit, Michigan, in August 2013. This initiative sought to examine how communities renowned for producing exceptional athletes could transfer that culture of excellence into the academic sphere. We held basketball skills instruction, workshops on college readiness and health, and panels discussing the relationship between sports and academics.

To further support youth development, we facilitated Conflict Resolution Education Workshops (CREW) in partnership with schools and youth programs in New York City and at Georgia Tech. These workshops incorporated conflict resolution education and art-based exercises to help young leaders constructively communicate and develop non-violent techniques to deal with everyday challenges.

In November 2013, we initiated the Career Pipeline Initiative at Booker T. Washington High School in Atlanta, GA. This program focused on career awareness and enrichment, fostering partnerships with schools, universities, and corporations. In 2015 and 2016, as part of the 3C Campaign (College, Career, & Civic Engagement), we partnered with the New York City Department of Education and College Summit. This comprehensive program aimed to impact the lives of middle and high school students by ensuring they were aware of their college options, inspired to pursue post-secondary education, equipped to attain employment, and civically engaged.

One of the highlights of the campaign was the Peer Leadership Conference held at the Barclays Center in Brooklyn, where students had the opportunity to engage with inspirational speakers, attend workshops on leadership and career development, and connect with mentors from various industries.

On January 27, 2016, we conducted college awareness assemblies in eight different New York City Middle Schools in partnership with the Department of Education and the City University of New York. These assemblies focused on providing information about college options, financial aid, and the importance of pursuing higher education. We aimed to inspire students to set ambitious goals for their future and empower them with the knowledge and resources to achieve those goals.

Additionally, during this time, we facilitated the establishment of the first Girls Who Code Club in the state of Georgia at Georgia State University in collaboration with students from Atlanta Booker T. Washington and George Washington Carver High Schools. This initiative aimed to bridge the gender gap in technology fields by providing young girls with opportunities to learn coding and computer science skills in a supportive environment.

Our commitment to promoting educational excellence and opportunities extended to other parts of the country as well. In 2015 and 2016, we partnered with the White House Initiative on Educational Excellence for African Americans, the California First Five Commission, and NAN Chapters in Los Angeles and Oakland to host Faith Leaders Trainings to Accelerate Early Learning Opportunities. These trainings brought together faith leaders, educators, and community organizations to discuss strategies for improving early childhood education and ensuring that young children had access to quality learning experiences.

Throughout these years, we continued to expand our Career Pipeline Initiative programming in South Florida with events and programming in Miami-Dade County and Broward County Public Schools. We conducted career awareness forums and workshops focusing on various fields such as criminal justice, business, entrepreneurship, communications, hospitality management, sports management, health, and STEM.

Our goal was to provide students with valuable insights into different career paths, help them explore their interests, and equip them with the necessary skills and knowledge to succeed in their chosen fields. We also facilitated workshops on career exploration, interviews, internships, and job placement, creating opportunities for students to gain real-world experience and connect with industry professionals.

These initiatives and partnerships were driven by our belief in the transformative power of education and the importance of equipping young people with the tools they need to succeed academically, professionally, and in their communities.

UNIVERSITY OF MASSACHUSETTS AMHERST EXPERIENCE

In the latter part of 2017, I was living in New York City and was very disgruntled. I had an appreciation for the subway but despised the over one-hour commute that I was making five days a week from Harlem, where I lived, to Crown Heights, Brooklyn, where I was an administrator at the City University of New York Medgar Evers College.

I also created a Brooklyn Saturday College Readiness Camp in part because I was also a lecturer on the faculty at the University of

Massachusetts Amherst, which was a three-hour drive from Harlem. It was primarily an online program, but I did have to be up there in person on Tuesday mornings for faculty meetings. It was a three-hour commute each way.

Two experiences from my time at UMass stand out for me. One was an act by one of my fellow faculty members to undermine me in a way that I had never before experienced. As I came to find out, this professor really wanted a friend of hers to be hired for the faculty opening instead of me. I remember her cold reaction to me as I interviewed in front of the whole faculty. The rest of the faculty went with me, but she apparently harbored some kind of grudge towards me.

I never missed a faculty meeting and handled all of my responsibilities, but unbeknownst to me, she was on a mission to get me out of there. She researched me vigorously and would try to bad mouth me to the program's director. She was finally able to get a breakthrough when she pressed the director into giving me an ultimatum and said that I would have to choose the University of Massachusetts or Medgar Evers College. I chose Medgar Evers College for the time being but was ultimately eyeing a return to South Florida.

As devious as I believed one faculty member to be, another showed me an incredible act of kindness. On one of my trips to Amherst, my car broke down as I went off on an exit to get an early morning sausage biscuit at a Burger King in a town just south of Hartford, Connecticut.

I remembered that one of my other fellow faculty members lived somewhere in Connecticut, and I gave her a call on the chance that she may have lived nearby because I knew that we were going to the same place for the faculty meeting. She did live in Connecticut, but it was over an hour away. She still found it in her heart to come and pick me up and take me to campus. It was an incredibly kind gesture, and it helped me realize that people are individuals and that I shouldn't typecast a whole group of people or people in a certain area in one way.

5000 ROLE MODELS OF EXCELLENCE PROJECT

My first day on the job with the 5000 Role Models of Excellence Project in April of 2018 was a memorable one. It began with a powerful demonstration of student activism at Miami Northwestern Senior High School. The students had walked out of their school and into the neighboring Liberty Square Housing Projects to protest gun violence in their community, grieving the loss of their classmates.

In a remarkable turn of events, the program's founder, Congresswoman Frederica Wilson, who was originally headed to the airport to fly to Washington D.C., redirected her driver to take her to Miami Northwestern instead. She wanted to speak with the students who organized the walkout and understand how she and her team could support their needs. I, along with another staff member, was invited to join the congresswoman at the school to engage with the student leaders and listen to their concerns about safety in their community.

The students expressed their desire for their issues to be taken as seriously as those voiced by students from more suburban areas, such as Parkland, Florida, where a tragic mass shooting had occurred earlier that year. One of the student leaders involved in the walkout was also a member of the 5000 Role Models chapter at the school. He went on to testify at a Congressional hearing on gun violence in Washington, D.C. the following month.

This impactful experience illustrated how Congresswoman Wilson leveraged her position to give these students a national platform to voice their concerns. I quickly realized the unique reach and structure of the 5000 Role Models program, with chapters spanning over 110 Miami-Dade County Public Schools, covering grades 3 to 12.

Recognizing the impossibility of individually reaching out to every student, I shifted my attention towards building relationships with the site directors who coordinated each school-based chapter. These site directors played a vital role in the size and functionality of each chapter, as they were often teachers, administrators, or other staff members.

The chapters provided various opportunities for the students, including field trips, weekly or bi-weekly meetings, and their own student leadership structure. Each chapter also had a group of mentors dedicated to supporting the boys' development. My responsibilities included recruiting mentors and facilitating their involvement in different 5000 Role Model students.

Additionally, the program organized "Teen Summits" at area hospitals, where multiple chapters would come together to hear from mentors and medical professionals. The program also hosted a Police and Youth Conference annually, creating a unique avenue for communication and understanding between law enforcement officers and the young men of the 5000 Role Models program.

Through role-playing scenarios, both the young men and the police officers gained a better understanding of each other's perspectives. The conference emphasized prevention, mutual respect, and constructive dialogue to improve the relationship between officers and young men. These interactions helped break down stereotypes, fostered empathy and improved communication. By promoting prevention measures and facilitating dialogue, the hope was to decrease the number of negative encounters between police and young men of color.

The Police and Youth Conference served as a platform for participating officers and departments to engage with 5000 Role Model students, demonstrating that they are not just enforcers but can also serve as supportive role models. The success of this collaborative effort could be replicated in cities across the country to improve relationships between law enforcement and communities, particularly among young men of color.

Furthermore, the 5000 Role Models program provided scholarships to select seniors called Wilson Scholars, helping cover the financial costs of attending college or university. Funds for the scholarships were raised during the annual Dr. Martin Luther King Jr. Scholarship Breakfast, a significant event drawing thousands of attendees.

Throughout his tenure, I had the opportunity to take groups of students to Washington, D.C., for various events, including the Congressional Black Caucus Annual Legislative Conference and the Congressional hearing on gun violence. These experiences allowed the students to engage in meaningful activism and witness the impact of their voices in national policymaking.

My time with the 5000 Role Models of Excellence Project was transformative. The program's commitment to empowering individuals and fostering productive communication left a lasting impression on me.

A GREAT PLAYBOOK FROM 5000 ROLE MODEL STUDENT GEORGE PICKENS

One of the many students that I had the pleasure of getting to know and mentor through the 5000 Role Models of Excellence Project is George Pickens. He is one of the most exemplary students and young men that I have ever come across. I chronicle some of the dedication, hard work, and strategic moves that I have seen him incorporate in a three-part series that I call "The Pickens Playbook":

The Pickens Playbook Part 1: 7 College Readiness Moves to Make for Student Success

Miami Northwestern Senior High is a school that is nationally known for producing some of the best football players and football teams in the country on a yearly basis. In 2021, the school produced one of the best all-around scholars in the country, George Pickens. He was not only the top-ranked academic student in the school, but he was also actively involved in extra-curricular leadership roles.

There is an old adage that says, "Success leaves clues." The tremendous academic success of George Pickens has left enough clues to formulate a playbook for others to follow. George's playbook is special because he has been able to execute in an environment that places extreme value on young Black males' ability to perform on the football field but not nearly as much on their ability to excel in other areas. Listed below are seven college readiness plays that George has implemented and are potentially scalable for broader populations of students:

1. Students should set goals and review them on a daily basis.

George said that the first thing that he does when he wakes up in the morning is look at his goals and a vision board that he has made. He looks at both his short-term goals and his long-term goals. This allows him to visualize what he wants to achieve and increases his belief in his ability to bring it to fruition.

Guiding and even requiring students to formulate and review their goals will increase their focus and help them see how their daily coursework connects to their broader aspirations. Training students to begin their days by looking within and making investments in their internal development is sure to pay dividends in the form of building the mental and spiritual strength to help them overcome adversity and persist in spite of challenges.

2. The elevation of academic achievement is key.

People generally do more and try harder in those areas where they are celebrated and valued. George recalled being celebrated at an end-of-year ceremony at his elementary school for being the top student in his grade. This encouragement helped to motivate him to continue to achieve at a high level.

The highlighting of academic excellence and the rewards of scholastic success should be put at the forefront with the same enthusiasm that achievement in sports is promoted. Kids growing up in Miami's urban neighborhoods have seen young men go from their same schools and circumstances and achieve National Football League (NFL) fame, fortune, and stardom.

They have seen institutions like the University of Miami and the University of Florida come into schools like Miami Northwestern Senior High School and see value in Black boys' ability to play football. These young men are recruited, pursued, and offered full scholarships.

The dream for them is real, and it seems very attainable. They see and know many examples of it. The same can be done for other routes.

3. Academic competition can generate elite performance.

George competed in math competitions and spelling bees through his involvement in the National Achievers Society since he was in the 6th grade. Group academic competitions like these were a key component to George's success that may differ from a lot of the traditional experiences of the masses of students. The process of training for these competitions with other students allowed George and others to have the opportunity to both challenge and encourage each other, similar to the way that members of a basketball or football team do. Peers push each other to heights that they may not have gotten to if they just trained by themselves.

Aspiring basketball players can do all the drills in the world by themselves. Still, they will never reach their full potential until they sharpen their craft against competitors that force them to make adjustments and tap into their creativity to get past opposition. The same is true for elite-level academic achievement. The Saturday academic practices and competitions were a key factor in George's scholastic acceleration, and they can be for others if more opportunities, venues, and infrastructures are made available.

Competition and celebration should be built around gatekeeper skillsets like math and crucial courses like Algebra. There is rightfully a great emphasis on science, technology, engineering, and mathematics (S.T.E.M.) careers, but S.T.E.M. will become STOP if students don't have the proficiency to pass high-level math classes.

Mechanisms that incentivize students to practice math like they practice basketball jump shots and football route running are needed.

This play from the Pickens playbook is sure to pay off in the long run, with more students being able to take advantage of opportunities in lucrative S.T.E.M. career fields.

4. Participation in sports can be a great developmental tool.

George played football in elementary and middle school for the Miami Gardens Ravens and recalls having fun with his friends. He described football as something that he always loved and was able to connect with. He has been able to translate many of the lessons that he learned on the football field into the classroom, like the importance of working hard and consistently practicing in order to produce winning results.

Though George enjoyed playing football, he never bought into the narrative that is dominant in the lives of so many young men that "football is their only way out." He resisted that characterization and didn't see himself as being one-dimensional. He maintained a more holistic definition of himself and embraced other leadership roles in extracurricular activities like being the President of the 5000 Role Models of Excellence Project Chapter at his school and the President of the South Florida National Achievers Society.

5. Dual Enrollment = Double Achievement

George began taking dual enrollment classes during the second semester of his freshman year with the goal of graduating with both a high school diploma and an Associate in Arts (AA) degree at the same time. He credits a member of his school's staff for making him aware of the dual enrollment option. The awareness of the availability of this opportunity was crucial as many students miss out on opportunities like dual enrollment because they are not provided information about it in a timely manner.

George's decision to take advantage of the dual enrollment opportunities that were made available to him through his high school and Miami Dade College was key to building additional momentum to keep him going. This momentum helped him to maximize his days and maintain the grueling daily regimen that this double-duty required. He would find periods during the day to do the necessary assignments and classwork. These time slots would be during breaks in classes, during lunch, commuting, and late at night when he got home from the Miami Dade College North Campus.

He was keenly aware that graduating with his high school diploma and AA degree simultaneously would give him a strong foundation and lay the groundwork for what he wanted to achieve in his life and the kind of impact that he wanted to make. This kind of awareness can build one's focus and push them to maintain the kind of habits and regimen that George was able to implement.

6. Career exploration helps to generate a sense of purpose.

George found a sense of purpose early in his life by seeing the issues that persisted in his community, like gun violence and unequal access to healthcare. It motivated him to want to be a part of the solution by becoming a medical doctor and social advocate. He considers himself to be a service-oriented person and relishes opportunities to lend a helping hand.

The medical magnet program at Northwestern was a part of his attraction to the school. The program introduces students to various careers in the medical field as early as the 9th grade, and they are also able to get industry certifications. Some of the teachers who teach the courses in the magnet program are also medical professionals, so they get instruction from those who are currently working in the field.

The importance of cultivating future healthcare professionals like George, who value treating of patients with care, compassion, and humanity, is vital. The COVID-19 pandemic and the restrictions around the family visitation of patients who are in the hospital have heightened the significance of how hospital personnel interact with patients. Hospital staff are now the only people in many cases that patients interact with, and they are dependent on them for company, motivation, and care while they are dealing with their affliction.

7. Mentorship and examples to emulate are critical.

One of the key infrastructures of opportunity that has benefitted George and thousands of others in Miami-Dade County is the 5000 Role Models of Excellence Project, a dropout prevention and mentorship program founded by U.S. Congresswoman Frederica Wilson in 1993. The program has chapters of boys in 110 schools in the county who receive mentorship, life skills training, and exposure to a myriad of different experiences, from health summits to prison visits to college tours to trips to Washington D.C. and more.

George joined the 5000 Role Models when he was in the 5th grade and has been a part of chapters at his elementary, middle, and high school. He became the President of the 5000 Role Models chapter at Miami Northwestern Senior High School. One of the most impactful experiences for George was a trip to a local prison where he came face to face with the realities of the mass incarceration epidemic and where the consequences of a bad decision or even being at the wrong place at the wrong time could lead him.

George appreciates the way that being a 5000 Role Model has helped to shape his character. It embodies brotherhood for him and has exposed him to various issues and careers within his community that he may have otherwise overlooked. Through the program, he has been able to have numerous speaking opportunities, including introducing President Barack Obama at a Miami rally in October 2020.

The brotherhood and positive peer pressure that is generated from programs like the 5000 Role Models has had an incalculable impact on the development of young men and should be institutionalized in school districts across the nation.

The development of life skills, character building, and quality decision-making are key factors that George acquired from other sources in addition to the 5000 Role Models. The primary source was his family. His late mother was an educator, and his father was a professional in the engineering field. They both emphasized the importance of education and the doors that it could open for him. His older sister was a stellar scholar and set a great example for him to follow and emulate.

This kind of family setup may not be replicable for the broader population of students, but there are other resources and infrastructures, like the 5000 Role Models of Excellence Project, that can be put in place to provide a consistent level of positive nurturing and support.

These seven plays from Pickens College Readiness Playbook can be adopted by other students and by systems and structures that are geared toward student development. It is important to note that this playbook does not guarantee success. It will not automatically give one the many intangible factors that George possesses and has consistently employed, like grit, determination, focus, discipline, and the ability to delay gratification, but it can serve as a starting point for transformational change.

The playbook for athletic excellence has been instilled, replicated, and institutionalized in the hearts and minds of young men of color and the communities that they inhabit. Playbooks for academic excellence can be embedded in the same way. Success is not guaranteed, but the combination of the right plays and the will to execute them are a formidable force to contend with. It is time to take a new look at what is working in our communities and schools and find innovative ways to scale them to broader populations of students so that they can be better prepared for access and success at higher education institutions.

The Pickens Playbook Part 2: Year One at Tennessee State University

It was the final week of April 2021, and the clock was running out for Miami Northwestern Senior High School Senior George Pickens to make his final decision on where he would be going to pursue higher education. Pickens, who graduated as the top-ranked student in his senior class, was the subject of a previous section entitled "The Pickens Playbook: 7 College Readiness Moves to Make for Student Success".

Pickens had many different choices, including Harvard University, Howard University, Duke University, and the University of Miami. Ultimately, he felt that he could not turn down the opportunity to go into the Bachelor of Science/Doctor of Medicine (BS/MD) Program at Tennessee State University (TSU), which included acceptance into the Meharry Medical College School of Medicine upon completion of his undergraduate work at TSU.

He was also impressed by the outreach and genuine efforts of the TSU administration following his visit to the campus in early April 2021. On his visit, he met with program staff and was given a personalized campus tour with Mr. and Ms. TSU. After he returned to Miami, personnel from the program called him every day to check up on him and give him guidance and support leading up to the May 1st decision deadline. He remarked that their persistence showed him how much they cared for students.

Pickens and his fellow cohort members of the Dr. Levi Watkins Jr. Accelerated Pathway Program (BS/MD students) arrived on campus in late July, a few weeks before the other students. They went to Meharry Medical College every day and heard testimonials from doctors and students. He described it as a two-week period of building connections and solidifying a long-term support system there. He also got a chance to build camaraderie with other members of his cohort.

After the orientation period, George was selected by an external organization, Baxter International, to receive scholarship support that would cover his enrollment through the completion of his medical school tenure after he matriculates to Meharry Medical College. These experiences helped to lay a solid foundation for an academic year that would end with him enjoying a great academic and social life balance on the TSU campus and finishing the academic year with a 4.0-grade point average. Below are some plays from the "Pickens Playbook" that helped him continue to build on his positive academic momentum at the collegiate level.

1. Remember why you came to college and remind yourself every day.

Pickens begins every day thinking about where he started and where he wants to go. He believes that this helps him to align with his mission and reconnects him to his faith. He stated, "I keep my mind focused on what I believe a big part of my purpose is to equip myself to be able to assist others on a daily basis and pour back into the community that poured into me. I become truly happy through service."

This mindset gives him the continuous motivation to put forth the consistent time, energy, and focus that is required for him to maintain his stellar grade point average. He challenges himself to be a better version of himself on that day than he was the previous day. He understands that he will have to work for what he wants and who he wants to become. Pickens expressed this by saying, "Success comes to those who work for it. It comes to those who wake up an hour earlier and stay up an hour later."

2. College is what you make of it.

Many students who will be matriculating to institutions of higher education will be experiencing a freedom that they had never previously had. They are essentially on their own to allocate their time and energy in whatever way they would like. It can understandably be difficult for people to be able to handle their newfound autonomy. Those who excel in this environment must be intentional about prioritizing their time and appropriately balancing their academic and social lives.

Every Sunday, Pickens creates a schedule for himself for the upcoming week with what he wants to accomplish and when he intends to do it. He then tries to stick as closely as he can to that schedule, though there are inevitably some things that come up that may cause him to deviate from what was planned. He understands and enjoys the social aspect of college life but has set a rule for himself that he must complete the academic work that he aims to achieve for the day before attending social events. He knows that it can be much more difficult to try to get this kind of work done after a late-night event on campus or somewhere else in the city.

3. Find a study routine that works for you.

Pickens knew that he would have to retool and redesign the study habits that he had in high school as he was transitioning into a different city, campus, and academic institution. He went through a trial-and-error process to see what worked and what didn't work in terms of maximizing his study time.

He initially tried studying in his room but found it to be not the most conducive for long-term concentration with his bed right there and other distractions readily available. He eventually settled on sequestering himself in a room in the library where he would put his phone on "do not disturb" for a few hours and see how much he could accomplish during that period of dedicated focus. He found this to work for him in a way that enabled him to establish a consistent daily routine where he could maximize his productivity during his planned study time.

4. Understand your place in history.

Pickens has a keen understanding of history and a deep appreciation for those who paved the way for him to have the opportunities that he is currently able to have. TSU, an institution that was founded on June 19, 1912, as the Tennessee Agricultural & Industrial State Normal School for Negroes and has long been a primary access point for students to continue their education and uplift their communities.

One hundred ten years after its founding, students like Pickens continue to build onto this legacy and blaze important traits, particularly in the field of medicine, where the percentage of Black male doctors in 2018 was 2.6%, and slightly under the 2.7% of Black male doctors in 1940. The production of more students like Pickens will be key to improving these numbers in the future.

Pickens is already a trailblazer by being the first student in the Class of 2021 from the 5000 Role Models of Excellence Project, a dropout prevention and mentorship program founded by Congresswoman Frederica Wilson, to secure a scholarship offer from TSU and ultimately commit to going. This helped to open the way for 11 other Florida-based students from the program to come in 2021 and an additional 42 students from the Class of 2022 who joined the following Fall.

The internal drive that Pickens has consistently generated within himself to produce successful outcomes in multiple areas of life is especially commendable. What Pickens has already accomplished has required day after day, week after week, and month after month of disciplined effort with minimal applause or celebration compared to other more celebrated pathways like athletics and entertainment.

His ability to delay gratification and remain focused on his purpose while taking the needed incremental steps of preparation to equip himself for excellence is worthy of study and is a large part of the basis of this evolving "playbook." The key to his external achievement has been his internal investment in his mental, spiritual, and intellectual development.

These plays from George Pickens include adjustments that students can incorporate to better prioritize their time and energy to have exceptional academic performance and still enjoy the social experience of college.

The Pickens Playbook Part 3: 2nd Year at Tennessee State University and MCAT Preparation

George Pickens is now in his third year at the institution and is on pace to finish his undergraduate studies at the conclusion of the Spring 2024 semester. During his second year, he faced the task of taking higher-level courses in his major during his second year at TSU. He found himself fully immersed in subjects like physics and organic chemistry.

During the Fall of 2022, he embraced the challenge head-on, immersing himself in these complex subjects. However, as the Spring semester arrived, he encountered an unexpected hurdle. He found himself enrolled in a difficult course that was taught by a professor with a strong accent that made it difficult for him to understand the lectures.

Now, Pickens had a choice: he could have chosen to complain about the professor's teaching style, hoping for change. But he made a calculated decision - he realized that engaging in a battle of that nature against a long-standing professor would not yield fruitful results.

Instead, George chose a different path. He decided to take matters into his own hands and get ahead of the challenges. He committed himself to teaching himself the lessons and sought external resources for further instruction. By doing this, he stayed multiple classes ahead of where the professor was. In essence, the class became a review for him, reinforcing concepts he had already mastered.

George's refusal to let this class impede his progress became his driving force. He understood that there would be other classes in the future where independent learning and supplementing class instruction would be necessary for mastery. George's success is a testament to the power of self-study and the determination to go above and beyond what is expected.

It is important to note that George's success did not come without hard work and dedication. He put in extra hours, pouring his energy into understanding the material deeply. He knew that in order to conquer the challenges ahead, he had to go above and beyond.

In addition to excelling in his coursework, George also put a strategic system of preparation in place for the upcoming MCAT. His preparation process consisted of three distinct phases:

- 1st Phase: A review of content that consisted of him recalling everything that he had learned and learning additional information that he needed to learn.

- 2nd Phase: Practicing problems online and through third parties and reviewing those that he got wrong and those that he got right by guessing.

- 3rd Phase: To test his knowledge and build up his stamina, George regularly took practice exams that simulated the conditions of the actual MCAT. This phase helped him identify areas of weakness and further refine his test-taking strategies.

George's dedication to MCAT preparation was evident through his study schedule. During the Spring semester, he studied 2 to 3 hours a night, utilizing prep books, flashcards, and practice problems. Throughout the summer, George increased his study time to 10 to 12 hours a day, including attending prep classes. Devoting around 2 hours to each topic, George covered multiple subjects daily, focusing on both content review and effective test-taking strategies.

George's remarkable efforts were supported by Tennessee State University and Meharry Medical College, who provided a system of preparation and support to nurture aspiring medical students. These institutions recognized the importance of guiding and preparing students like George for success in medical school.

George Pickens' journey toward conquering the MCAT showcases the power of determination, self-study, and strategic preparation. Facing challenges head-on and taking responsibility for his own learning, George exemplifies the resilience necessary for success in the medical field. With the support of Tennessee State University and Meharry Medical College, George is well-equipped to pursue his dreams of becoming a medical professional.

RISING COACHES DEI ALLIANCE

In the summer of 2020, in the aftermath of the tragic killing of George Floyd, I was approached by Adam Gordon, the founder of Rising Coaches, to speak at a virtual meeting for college basketball coaches and administrators. The purpose of the meeting was to explore the intersection of athletics and social justice, as these individuals were grappling with the events unfolding in the country and how to address the emotions of their players and themselves.

As I joined the call, I was struck by the impressive turnout, with over 300 coaches and administrators participating. I was invited to speak due to my background in activism and sports writing, and the impact of sports on society became even more evident during that call. I pondered the influence that coaches and institutions have not only on their student-athletes but also on their campuses and surrounding communities. I realized that sports, both on and off the court or field, had immense potential as a vehicle for social change.

Adam and others recognized that this moment needed to be transformed into a lasting movement, so they established the Rising Coaches DEI (Diversity, Equity, and Inclusion) Alliance. This alliance consisted of twelve college basketball organizations focused on minority representation and social justice coaching. These organizations included Coaches for Change, Asian Coaches Association, Women of Color Coaches Network, Jewish Coaches Association, Equality Coaching Alliance, Minority Coaches Association, EmbraceUs, Latino Association of Basketball Coaches, Black Coaches United, Black Coaches Association, Coaches For Action, and Be Ready Family.

They understood that once the initial fervor subsided, the focus would primarily return to winning games. Therefore, they recognized the need for a lasting framework to continue driving progress forward. In December of that year, Adam approached me to join as a senior advisor for the alliance, and I gladly accepted. Together, we began planning what would later become known as the Equality and Inclusion Games in college basketball.

During the month of February, over 150 Division I men's and women's basketball programs designated a specific game dedicated to uplifting the importance of equality and inclusion. These games provided a platform for players, coaches, and programs to address social justice issues they were passionate about. Many institutions also used this opportunity to expand programming across their campuses.

This campaign presented a great opportunity to use the platform of college basketball to channel the focus, attention, and energy of student-athletes, coaches, administrators, and fan bases on important societal issues. It was also an opportunity to reassert the common humanity of student-athletes in a way that went beyond their performance on the court and into who they are, where they are from, what they care about, and what issues may be important to their communities of origin.

After the campaign, I created the design and implementation plan for an Empowerment Series that partnered with college and university athletic departments to provide on-campus workshops for athletic departments, coaching staff, student-athletes, and the broader community. These workshops aimed to expose participants to emerging career paths, financial literacy, blockchain technology, building and monetizing student-athlete brands, and mindset training.

The Rising Coaches DEI Alliance also launched the "Next Up Initiative," which involved each participating organization nominating a men's and women's assistant coach who showed potential to become a head coach. We partnered with a search firm to conduct mock interviews, helping these coaches prepare for the next step in their careers. Several participants in this initiative have since secured head coaching positions.

The alliance and the initiatives it undertook have demonstrated the power of sports in facilitating social change. By leveraging the influence of coaches and institutions, we can create a more inclusive and equitable environment both on and off the court. Sports provide a unique platform to address important societal issues, and the Rising Coaches DEI Alliance continues to drive forward its mission to promote diversity, equity, and inclusion in college basketball and beyond.

THE TRANSFORMATIVE IMPACT OF MY WIFE

When I met my wife in November of 2020, my life changed forever. She is absolutely tailor-made for me. It is rare when life exceeds your dreams. With Angelina, it certainly has. She possesses an inner and outer beauty that takes my breath away. She is beautiful, incredibly driven, inspirational, resilient, dynamic, and spiritually guided. I am so grateful to have her as my life partner and to love and be loved by her.

Angelina is a force to be reckoned with - a woman who fearlessly pursues her dreams and sets an example for others to follow. Her resilience in the face of challenges is awe-inspiring, reminding me to never give up even when the odds seem insurmountable.

What truly sets Angelina apart is her dynamic nature. She is not limited by society's expectations or confined by anyone's perception of who she should be. Instead, she embraces her uniqueness and allows her spirit to soar. Her ability to create systems for herself and others and her ability to adapt to any situation amazes me. Through her own journey of self-discovery, she has taught me the importance of embracing change and stepping out of my comfort zone.

But perhaps the most significant aspect of our relationship is the spiritual connection we share. Angelina is guided by a deep sense of faith and spirituality that permeates every aspect of her life. Her steadfast belief in a higher power has allowed her to navigate life's challenges with grace and gratitude. Through her strong faith, she has opened my eyes to a new level of understanding and purpose that I never thought possible.

I am eternally grateful to have Angelina as my life partner, my confidante, and my best friend. Her presence in my life has uplifted me, inspired me, and propelled me to new heights. May our journey together continue to be filled with love, growth, and endless possibilities.

Marcus Al

In many ways, I wrote this book for my son Marcus Al. This book is a blueprint for how individuals can fulfill their purpose and how we can transform parts of our society that need corrective action. This is certainly applicable to my son.

I am filled with pride and excitement as I watch Marcus Al embark on this new chapter of his life. Kindergarten is just the beginning of his incredible journey, one where he will undoubtedly leave his own unique imprint on our society. The knowledge and values that he acquires along the way will shape him into a compassionate, responsible, and influential individual who will make a positive impact on the world.

As a father, I seek to provide Marcus Al with a strong foundation that instills values such as integrity, empathy, and perseverance, and I am grateful for the strong support system that he has to help guide him.

Marcus Al has an extremely bright future ahead, and it is my hope that this book will serve as a source of inspiration and motivation for him, reminding him of the potential that he possesses and the impact he can make. I want him to know that his actions matter, that his voice can be heard, and that he has the ability to shape a better world for himself and generations to come. To Marcus Al and the entire generation of children who will inherit the world we leave them, may this book be a guiding star, illuminating their path as they navigate through life.

Together, let us bridge divides, challenge outdated systems, and build a society that values the inherent worth and potential of every individual. In doing so, we will pave the way for lasting transformation, improving the quality of life for people everywhere. It is time to turn our collective gaze toward the horizon, where the bridges we construct today will lead us toward a world of greater equity, compassion, and justice.

Like Dr. Martin Luther King Jr., sixty years ago on the steps of the Lincoln Memorial, let us dare to dream, to envision a world that is yet to be, and to share our dreams with others. Together, we can build a future that exceeds our wildest imaginations. Our dreams have the power to transform our lives, our communities, and our world.

REFERENCES

Council of Chief State School Officers. (2017). *Birth to grade 3 indicator framework: Opportunities to integrate early childhood in ESSA toolkit.* https://ccsso.org/resource-library/birth-grade-3-indicator-framework-opportunities-integrate-early-childhood-essa

Council of Economic Advisers. (2014). *The economics of early childhood investments.* The White House. https://obamawhitehouse.archives.gov/sites/default/files/docs/the_economics_of_early_childhood_investments.pdf

Kingdon, J. W. (1984). *Agendas, alternatives and public policies.* Pearson Education.

Lipsky, M. (1980). *Street-level bureaucracy: Dilemmas of the individual in public services.* Russell Sage Foundation.

Miller, H. T. (2012). *Governing narratives: Symbolic politics and policy change.* University Of Alabama Press.

O'Neil, D. (2012). *Isiah Thomas hire was a joke from the start.* Men's College Basketball Blog. https://www.espn.com/blog/collegebasketballnation/post/_/id/57620/isiah-thomas-hire-was-a-joke-from-the-start

Rovner, J. (2021). *Black disparities in youth incarceration.* The Sentencing Project. https://www.sentencingproject.org/fact-sheet/black-disparities-in-youth-incarceration/

Volker, A. M. (2011). The mary howard health center: Meeting the health care needs of the chronically homeless in philadelphia.

Social Innovations, *8.* https://socialinnovationsjournal.org/social-issues/95-health/1872-the-mary-howard-health-center-meeting-the-health-care-needs-of-the-chronically-homeless-in-philadelphia

Warner, T. C., Avalos, M., Ye, S., Mercado, D., Cordova, J., & Marshall, B. **(2023).** *Trends in youth arrests in miami-dade county: 2010-2022.* Miami-Dade Economic Advocacy Trust; University of Miami School of Education & Human Development.

ABOUT THE AUTHOR

D r. Marcus Bright is an author, social impact leader, and nationally renowned speaker. As a scholar, former college athlete, university professor, government administrator, foundation executive, and community change agent, Dr. Bright has had nearly two decades of experience working with institutions, organizations, and communities to build partnerships and put processes in place that generate access, opportunities, and resources for socioeconomic mobility.

His first book, "Brighter Ways Forward: Reflections on Sports, Tech, and Socioeconomic Mobility," features an in-depth exploration of the role of sports and tech and how they can be leveraged for socioeconomic mobility. It spans many social issues and contains a multifaceted analysis of problems in each area and recommendations and strategies for progress and solutions. He has published over 150 articles in numerous publications, including the Huffington Post, The Grio, Diverse: Issues in Higher Education, and the Miami Herald and has spoken across the country on a variety of topics related to public policy, education, and social justice.

As the Senior Advisor for the Rising Coaches Diversity, Equity, and Inclusion (DEI) Alliance, which is made up of a dozen social justice and minority coaching organizations and is among the largest organized groups of basketball coaches in the World, he helped lead an "Equality and Inclusion Campaign" across college basketball that included partnerships with over 150 colleges and universities.

He served as district administrator for the 5000 Role Models of Excellence Project, a school-system-based dropout prevention and mentorship program that served thousands of boys for four years and has held administrative posts at Florida International University, City University of New York Medgar Evers College, Miami-Dade County Economic Advocacy Trust, and the Miami-Dade County Public Schools Office of Educational Equity, Access, and Diversity.

He served as Executive Director of Education for a Better America (EBA), a non-profit organization that partnered with school districts, universities, churches, and community organizations in over 15 cities across the nation to conduct educational programming and enhance public policy engagement. Dr. Bright previously taught at Florida International University, Lynn University, City University of New York Medgar Evers College, Florida Atlantic University, and the University of Massachusetts Amherst.

He received a Ph.D. in Public Administration from Florida Atlantic University, a Master's Degree in Public Administration from Florida International University, and a Bachelor's Degree in Government and World Affairs from the University of Tampa.